James Weldon Johnson
Songwriter

Don Cusic

Cover Design:
Steve Laughbaum

Layout/Creative Design:
Julie Price
Priceless Design

Production Coordinator:
Jim Sharp,
Sharp Management

Dedication

This book is dedicated to Mike Curb
and the Mike Curb Family Foundation,
without whom it would not have
been possible.

Acknowledgments

Sheet music to most of the songs written by James Weldon Johnson is found in the Beinecke Library at Yale and I am greatly indebted to their help in making those available. I also found copies of sheet music at the Center for Popular Music at Middle Tennessee State University in Murfreesboro, Tennessee, and on various web sites. The Belmont and Fisk University Libraries were also a great help and I am indebted to Belmont University for their continued support of my work. My deepest thanks goes to Mike Curb and the Mike Curb Foundation, who provided a Professorship for me at Belmont University, which allows me to undertake projects such as this one on James Weldon Johnson.

Introduction

During the period 1900-1906, long before James Weldon Johnson was known as one of the most prominent African-Americans in the United States, he was a member of one of the most successful and well-known songwriting teams in New York, writing hits for stage musicals.

As a songwriter, James Weldon Johnson is best known for "Lift Every Voice and Sing," which became known as "The Negro National Anthem" and continues to be performed by African-American choirs. Johnson's fame as a songwriter has been eclipsed by his work in Civil Rights—he was the first African-American head of the National Association of Colored People (NAACP), as a novelist (*The Autobiography of an Ex-Colored Man*), poet (*God's Trombones*) and educator (he finished his career as a distinguished professor at Fisk University in Nashville).

Except for "Lift Every Voice," it is rare to hear a recording of a James Weldon Johnson song because he wrote during the era of sheet music, so most of his songs have not been heard for over 100 years. Popular songs of the late nineteenth and early twentieth century were known as "ragtime" and many were known as "coon songs," which are grim reminders of the blatant racism of the late nineteenth and early twentieth centuries. Johnson and his songwriting partners, his brother Rosamond Johnson and Bob Cole, wrote a number of songs that have been labeled "coon songs" but the trio always sought to rise above the denigration of blacks and yet remain commercial. However, the fact remains that many of the songs that Bob Cole and the Johnsons wrote fit the definition of "coon songs."

A number of other African-American songwriters also wrote "coon songs" because, during that time, they were popular and successful songwriters have to write songs that fit the times and the audience.

Cole and the Johnson Brothers wrote songs for musicals presented to white audiences, although they were part of a group of African-American songwriters and performers who placed their works at the forefront of black culture. Although their songs have, for the most part, been forgotten and buried in the past, they are remarkably strong, vibrant and some fit easily into the twenty-first century. Although some of the lyrics seem objectionable, for the most part Cole and the Johnson Brothers succeeded in elevating the Negro of the early twentieth century above many of the racist images of the day.

James Weldon Johnson: Background

James William Johnson—he adapted "Weldon" later—was born June 17, 1871 in Jacksonville, Florida. His mother, a public school teacher and accomplished musician, taught him and his brother, John Rosamond Johnson (born August 11, 1873) to play piano, although Jim, as he was known, preferred the guitar. In 1894 Johnson graduated from Atlanta University and taught at a small, rural school in Georgia, then moved back to Jacksonville where, at the age of 23, he became principal of Stanton, a school for African-American students. During his tenure at Stanton, Johnson extended the school from eight to ten grades.

In 1897, Johnson passed the bar exam and became the first African-American admitted to the Florida bar. After Johnson passed the bar, his brother, Rosamond, who had studied music at the New England Conservatory of Music in Boston and was teaching at the Baptist Academy in Jacksonville, approached him with the idea of writing a comic opera. They decided on a story that satirized American imperialism, set on a Pacific island, and worked on it for about a year before it was finished. Titled *Tolsa*, they played it for their friends in Jacksonville and, encouraged by the response, decided to go to New York in the summer of 1899 and attempt to get it produced on Broadway. The country was still gripped with "war fever" from the Spanish-American War in 1898 so a war theme was popular.

The Johnson brothers managed to audition the show for Isadore Witmark at the music publisher M. Witmark and Sons. Whitmark was impressed but decided to pass; however, the Johnsons met many of the stars and producers of comic opera and musical plays in New York.

The Johnsons arrived in New York at an opportune time and James Weldon Johnson observed that "The close of the nineties and the following decade was the high-watermark period of the coloured writers of popular songs in New York."[1]

Black Entertainers in the Late Nineteenth Century

The Fisk Jubilee Singers, and other similar gospel groups, had toured regularly since the 1870s. In 1890, Sam T. Jack organized *The Creole Show*, which featured beautiful young African-American women with a line-up similar to a minstrel show. In 1896 The Black Patti Troubadours was formed by Sissieretta Jones, an African-American concert singer who was not allowed to perform on many concert stages. Her managers, Voelckel and Nolan, formed the show, which featured vaudeville and popular songs. At the end of the evening, a short concert of operatic airs was performed by Jones, known as the "Black Patti" because she was compared to Andelina Patti, the leading Italian opera singer of that time.

The comedy team of Williams and Walker arrived in New York in 1896 and was an immediate hit on the vaudeville stage. Within a decade, Bert Williams became the top African-American comedian and then joined Ziegfeld's Follies. In April, 1898, *A Trip to Coontown*, starring Bob Cole and Billy Johnson, opened in New York and is generally considered to be the first critically acknowledged black musical comedy. In July of that year, *Clorindy, or The Origin of the Cakewalk*, considered to be the first black show staged in a Broadway theater, premiered in New York. Will Marion Cook composed the music for *Clorindy* and Paul Laurence Dunbar wrote the libretto and lyrics, although Ernest Hogan, who starred in the show, re-wrote much of the libretto and lyrics. In 1899 *Jes' Lak White Folks* by Cook and Dunbar premiered.

Ernest Hogan

Ernest Hogan wrote the song "All Coons Look Alike To Me" in 1896, which started a craze in "coon songs." "Coon songs" were songs whose lyrics stereotyped African-Americans as being laughable, comic, lazy, shiftless creatures given to excesses and vices. Songwriters—black and white-- took ragtime rhythms and added lyrics in black dialect, stereotyping blacks into several broad categories. In addition to the lyrics, sheet music covers further perpetuated stereotypes of blacks. The covers pictured blacks with full, large lips, rolling eyes, or dandified dress indicating they were socially out of place.

Ernest Hogan, born Reuben Crowders in Bowling Green, Kentucky shortly after the end of the Civil War, began performing in tent shows and minstrel shows during his teen years. He took the stage name "Ernest Hogan" and by 1891 he lived in Chicago, where he was co-owner of Eden and Hogan's Minstrels. In 1896 Hogan was living in New York when he wrote "All Coons Look Alike to Me," which was published in August after arranger Max Hoffman added an extra syncopated chorus. In that song, Hogan had "accidentally capsulized one of the baser tenants of prejudice, that all blacks are alike and need not be thought of or dealt with as individuals." The song set off "an explosion of coonery in pop songs" and over a million copies of the sheet music were sold over the next few years as the song "became the specialty number of many vaudeville singers"[2]

In his autobiography, *Along This Way*, James Weldon Johnson described Ernest Hogan as "expansive, jolly, radiating infectious good humor; provoking laughter merely by the changing expressions of his mobile face—a face that never, even on the stage, required cork or paint to produce comical effects."[3]

All Coons Look Alike to Me

Talk about a coon a having trouble
I think I have enough of ma own
It's alla bout ma Lucy Jane Stubbles
And she has caused my heart to mourn
Thar's another coon barber from Virginia
In soci'ty he's the leader of the day
And now ma honey gal is gwine to quit me
Yes she's gone and drove this coon away
She'd no excuse to turn me loose
I've been abused, I'm all confused
Cause these words she did say

Chorus:
All coons look alike to me
I've got another beau, you see
And he's just as good to me as you, nig!
Ever tried to be
He spends his money free,
I know we can't agree
So I don't like you no how
All coons look alike to me

Never said a word to hurt her feelings
I always bou't her presents by the score
And now my brain with sorrow am a reeling
Cause she won't accept them any more
If I treated her wrong she may have loved me
Like all the rest she's gone and let me down
If I'm lucky I'm a gwine to catch my policy
And win my sweet thing way from town
For I'm worried, yes, I'm desp'rate

I've been Jonahed, and I'll get dang'rous
If these words she says to me

All coons look alike to me
I've got another beau, you see
And he's just as good to me as you, nig!
Ever tried to be
He spends his money free,
I know we can't agree
So I don't like you no how
All coons look alike to me

"All Coons Look Alike to Me" became popular during the time that Ernest Hogan was on the road, touring with the Georgia Graduates company. When he returned to New York in 1897 he became the comedian with Black Patti's Troubadours.

"Coon songs" caused controversy and problems within the African-American community. An editorial in the *Indianapolis Freeman*, an African-American newspaper, noted that "Colored men in general took no offense at the proceedings and laughed as heartily on hearing a 'coon' song as the whites. But where the rub came is when the colored man was called a 'coon' outside of the opera house." The editorial continued:

"The name 'coon' in a song, we understand, is only meant as an assumed name, just to amuse or cause laughter while you are hearing the song or seeing the play; but it don't stop there. A show goes to a country town—some low down, loud-mouth "coon shouter" sings 'Coon, Coon, Coon,' or some other song that has plenty of 'coon' in it, with an emphasis on the word 'coon.' Then the people, especially the children, are educated that a colored man is a 'coon.' What was meant for a jest is taken seriously. Before the show came the people were afraid to call a black man a 'coon.' Or they may have wanted to show him some respect by calling him 'colored.' But now they think it's all right and he won't mind, because it's all in fun and it's in all the songs. In this way and many other ways too numerous to mention, 'coon' songs have done more to insult the Negro and caused his white brethren, especially the young generation, to have a bad opinion of good Negroes as well as bad Negroes, than anything that has ever happened."[4]

Williams and Walker

On their first trip to New York the Johnsons met Bert Williams and George Walker of the "Williams and Walker" vaudeville team. During his career Bert Williams was described as "not just a star: he was the sun" [who] "drew every major black composer, lyricist, and librettist of his time into his orbit. All wrote for him, some wrote with him, and many of them flourished in his light as they never would again."[5]

Egbert Austin "Bert" Williams was born on November 12, 1875 in Nassau, the Bahamas, and moved with his family to Florida, then to Riverside, California. After high school, Williams moved to San Francisco and in 1893 joined Martin and Selig's Mastodon Minstrels, where he teamed with George Walker for a few skits and the two soon became partners.

George Walker, a year older than Williams, was a dancer from Lawrence, Kansas and the duo featured Williams as the straight man with Walker providing the comedy; however, during their early partnership the roles were reversed. Williams and Walker toured as "The Two Real Coons" with Williams playing the "Jim Crow" character while George Walker played "Zip Coon."

(Three characters emerged in black face. "Jim Crow" was a shuffling, ignorant, naïve black; "Zip Coon" was a dandy, always pretending to rise above is social state; and "Sambo" was a comedic preacher whose sermons stereotyped black Christianity as witless and misguided.)

In 1896 Williams and Walker were urged to go to New York to audition for *The Gold Bug*, an operetta by Victor Herbert but George Lederer, the co-producer, was not impressed. However, when *The Gold Bug* opened on Broadway in September, the play was a flop, so Lederer contacted Williams and Walker, who did their regular vaudeville routine during the performance; it was a knockout. In *The Gold Bug*, Williams sang a song he wrote, "Oh! I Don't Know,

You're Not So Warm!"

The high point of their act was a comic version of "The Cake-walk," a new dance fad. According to David Jasen and Gene Jones in their book, *Spreadin' Rhythm Around: Black Popular Songwriters, 1880-1930,* "The cakewalk was an exuberant, high-stepping strut, the immediate descendent of the old minstrel show walk around... The opportunity for dancing in couples inspired the improvisational teamwork of the cakewalk and added a sexual frisson to black variety...It was the first black 'crossover' dance, and Williams and Walker crossed over with it."[6] Williams and Walker were a hit, but *The Gold Bug* was not; it closed after a week but it launched the New York careers of Williams and Walker.

During the 1893 World's Fair in Chicago, Williams and Walker performed as members of the Dahomey Village. The African nation of Dahomey was in the news after it resisted French colonial rule and, under King Behanzin, captured a number of Europeans as hostages to counter a French attack. When the French attacked, the Dahomeans fought valiantly but the French gained control of the region by 1894.

The battle for self-rule was not the only reason that Dohemy was in the American and European news; it "became infamous for its putative rituals of human sacrifice and cannibalism. While reports spoke of unwilling Europeans made witness to King Behanzin's chilling rituals, later displays at expositions brought the 'savages' home to intrigued Americans. It made perfect sense to them to present the barbaric backward peoples to crowds gathered at fairs while also celebrating America's unstoppable progress as the shining light of the World."[7]

In Chicago, Williams and Walker appeared in the all-black production, *The Octoroons,* which was based on the traditional minstrel show format but discarded the end men and included a chorus line. Other actors and musicians in *The Octoroons* were Bob Cole, Jesse Shipp, Will Marion Cook and Will Accooe.

Bert Williams performed in black face during his entire career, The Mask "removed all traces of the dignified young man he was, replacing himself with the woeful darkey who would sing about the coldness of his beloved." According to Williams' biographer Camille Forbes, "instead of being trapped inside the mask, he viewed it as 'a great protection...I shuffle onto the stage, not as myself, but as a lazy, slow-going negro'...Burnt cork became part of what enabled him to step into that onstage self, the buffer between the audience and the inner Williams."[8]

In his autobiography, James Weldon Johnson described Williams as "tall and broad-shouldered; on the whole, a rather handsome figure, and entirely unrecognizable as the shambling, shuffling 'darky' he impersonated on the stage; luxury-loving and indolent, but highly intelligent and with a certain reserve which at times exhibited itself as downright snobbishness; talking with a very slow drawl and getting more satisfaction, it seemed, out of being considered a great raconteur than out of being a great comedian; extremely funny in his imitations in the West Indian dialect."[9]

Johnson noted that Bert's wife, Lottie, told better stories, all "centered around one character, and that character was Bert. She recited very comically—the comicality heightened by her prettiness—her trials and tribulations with Bert on the 'road,' the chief of them being the many devices to which she had to resort to get him out of bed in time to catch early trains."[10]

Johnson described George Walker as "very black, very vigorous, and very dapper, being dressed always a point or two above the height of fashion. George, the hail-fellow-well-met, the mixer, the diplomat; frequently flashing that celebrated row of gleaming teeth in making his way to his objective; but serious withal and the driving force of the famous team; working tirelessly to convince New York managers that Negro companies should be booked in first-class houses, and, finally, succeeding."[11]

Aida Overton, George Walker's wife, was described by Johnson as "not as good-looking as Lottie Williams, but more than making up for what she lacked in looks by her remarkable talent; a wonderful dancer, and the possessor of a low-pitched voice with a natural sob to it, which she knew how to use with telling effect in 'Putting over' a song; beyond comparison, the brightest star among women on the Negro stage of the period, and hardly a lesser attraction of the Williams and Walker company than the two comedians."[12]

Bob Cole

On their first trip to New York the Johnson brothers also met Bob Cole, "one of the most talented and versatile Negroes ever connected with the stage," wrote Johnson. "He could write a play, stage it, and play a part. Although he was not a trained musician, he was the originator of a long list of catchy songs."[13]

Robert Allen Cole was born on July 1, 1868 in Athens, Georgia, son of a carpenter who was a local political figure. There was music in the home with informal musical get-togethers. During his teens, Cole lived in Jacksonville, Florida with relatives before he moved with his family to Atlanta, where he attended Atlanta University, but did not graduate. During the 1890s Cole left Atlanta and began his show business career in vaudeville with partner Lew Henry. He was based in Chicago by 1890 and joined the original Creole Show Company where he met singer-dancer Stella Wiley, who he later married.

In the Creole Company, Cole served as a singer, dancer and monologist as well as director; he also began writing songs. His first two songs, "Parthenia Took a Fancy to a Coon" and "In Shin Bone Alley" were published by Chicago publisher Will Rossiter in 1883.

Cole and Wiley toured out of Chicago but in 1894, at the age of 26, Cole decided to produce his own shows so he and Stella moved to New York where he founded the All Star Stock Company at Worth's Museum, located at Sixth Avenue and Thirtieth Street. The company conducted classes and workshops for young black actors and writers; however, the company folded after a few months in 1895.

One of Cole's students, Billy Johnson, a veteran of minstrel shows, was from Charleston, South Carolina. Johnson was ten years older than Cole and in 1881 wrote the song "The Trumpet in the Cornfield." He had been in New York since 1887 and performed with the Hicks-Sawyer Minstrels. When Cole's company disbanded, Johnson joined John W. Isham's Original Octoroons Show while

Bob Cole and Stella returned to the Creole Show. In 1896, Cole and Johnson joined the Black Patti Troubadours, where they served as comedians and writers. Their one-act sketch, "At Jolly Coon-ey Island" was successful, with Johnson playing a bunco artist, "Jim Flimflammer" while Cole was "Willie Wayside," a tramp in white-face. Songs they sang included "The Black Four Hundred's Ball," "Red Hots" and "Song of the Bathers." During the winter of 1896-1897, their "Coon-ey Island" was a popular skit with the Black Patti Troubadours.

The Black Patti Troubadours had an extended run in New York at Proctor's Fifty-eighth Street Theater where, in June, 1897, Cole asked owners Voelckel and Nolen for a raise; they refused so Cole took his score of songs written for the show and left. Arrested for theft, Cole landed in court where he established legal ownership of his music; however, the Court ruled that while Cole would be paid for the use of his music, the Troubadours kept the right to use his score in their show. When Cole left the show, Johnson also left and was replaced by Ernest Hogan, who performed in a re-written version of "At Jolly Coon-ey Island."[14]

Bob Cole and Billy Johnson formed a team and, spurred by Cole's ambition to write his own shows, wrote a two-act musical in 1897. The musical, *A Trip to Coontown*, was first performed in September, 1897 in a theater in South Amboy, New Jersey. This was "the first full-length musical comedy to be produced, written, staged, and performed by blacks."[15]

A Trip to Coontown was modeled on *In Gay New York* and *In Gayest Manhattan,* which were "sightseeing shows." The musical featured the songs "When the Chickens Go to Sleep," "4-11-44," "No Coons Allowed," "The Wedding of the Chinee and the Coon," and "I Hope These Few Lines Will Find You Well." Cole and Johnson had a difficult time staging their show because Voelckel and Nolan threatened theater owners by refusing to book the Black Patti Troubadours in any theater that booked *A Trip to Coontown*. However, Cole and Johnson struggled on and, after a tour of Canada, opened their show in April, 1898 in New York at Jacobs' Third Avenue

Theater. The show went on a successful tour and returned to New York in Spring, 1899 with performances at the Casino Roof Garden and the Grand Opera House.[16]

African-American theater was blossoming in New York; by 1899, *Clorindy, Jes'Lak White Folks* and three Williams and Walker shows were staged.

A Trip to Coontown stayed on the road for most of 1900 but the Cole-Johnson partnership was coming apart; Bob Cole was looking to write with someone other than Billy Johnson when he met James Weldon and J. Rosamond Johnson.

The Johnson Brothers in New York

The Johnsons attended rehearsals for two productions by Negro companies and enjoyed the nightlife in Negro Bohemia in the "Tenderloin" district, located between Sixth and Seventh Avenues around 28th Street, during their first trip to New York. In his autobiography, *Along This Way*, Johnson observes that "These glimpses of life" seen during their last few weeks in New York "were not wholly unfamiliar to Rosamond, but they showed me a new world—an alluring world, a tempting world, a world of greatly lessened restraints, a world of fascinating perils; but, above all, a world of tremendous artistic potentialities. Up to this time, outside of polemical essays on the race question, I had not written a single line that had any relation to the Negro. I now began to grope toward a realization of the importance of the American Negro's cultural background and his native folk-art, and to speculate on the superstructure of conscious art that might be reared upon them."[17]

At the end of that first summer in New York, Bob Cole and the Johnsons wrote "Louisiana Lize" and sold the singing rights to May Irwin for $50, the first money they earned as songwriters.

During this period, several white women—usually with a buxom figure--performed African-American songs in a style mimicking African-American performers. They were known as "coon shouters" and among these were May Irwin, Marie Cahill, Elizabeth Murray, Stella Mayhew, Artie Hall, and Clarice Vance. African-American performers such as Bessie Smith, Ma Rainey, Carrie Hall, Bessie Gillam and Rosa Scott were also known as "coon shouters" before they were called "blues" singers.

Back to Jacksonville

After that first summer in New York, James and Rosamond Johnson returned to Jacksonville and resumed their teaching careers. Johnson continued his work as principal at Stanton and Rosamond continued teaching music at the Baptist Academy. James wrote several poems, including "Lift Every Voice and Sing," which Rosamond set to music for a special program on the anniversary of President Abraham Lincoln's birthday on February 12, 1900. The song was performed by a children's chorus and, after the performance, the Johnsons forgot about the song "but the schoolchildren of Jacksonville kept singing the song; some of them went off to other schools and kept singing it; some of them became schoolteachers and taught it to their pupils," remembered James Johnson.[18] The song spread rapidly and was later adopted by the National Association for the Advancement of Colored People; it continues to be performed.

When the school year ended in late Spring, 1900, the Johnson brothers made their second trip to New York. During the school year, Rosamond's work with the Baptist Academy and James's work at school and with his law practice took up much of their time, so they did not have the opportunity to work on songs. However, back in New York they re-united with Bob Cole and the three formed a partnership to write songs and plays. It was a unique working arrangement and Johnson noted that "I have not known of just such another combination as was ours. The three of us sometimes worked as one man. At such times it was difficult to point out specifically the part done by any one of us. But, generally, we worked in a pair, with the odd man as a sort of critic and adviser. Without regard to who or how many did the work, each of us received a third of the earnings. There was an almost complete absence of pride of authorship; and that made the partnership still more curious. At first, we printed the three names at the top of the sheet, but three names on little songs looked top heavy; so we began printing only two; sometimes we printed but one."[19]

Although Johnson made that claim in his autobiography, each song credits specific writers, possibly a result of their publisher's desire to know the contribution of each of the writers and give appropriate credit. It is also possible that Johnson, who wrote this thirty years after their songwriting days were over, wanted to receive credit for songs where he had input but his name was not on the sheet music.

During this period in American theater, songs were often "interpolated" into musicals. Since a musical needed hit songs, a singer was always on the look-out for catchy material; if the song drew good audience response (and sold sheet music) then it was added to the score. A musical at that time generally had a story line but the songs were not integral to the plot. Cole and the Johnson Brothers were in demand to write songs that were a hit with the audience, regardless of the storyline of the musical.

(The practice of interpolating songs into musicals ended in 1924 when ASCAP ruled that musicals could only use the songs of the composer. After this point, song pluggers, publishers and songwriters were no longer allowed to push to have their songs added to a musical.)

By the end of that summer, Cole and the Johnson brothers had achieved success in getting their songs into shows, but had not made much money; they had to borrow money to return to Jacksonville where, during the following school year, Rosamond's music students and James' job as principal of Stanton took up most of their time. Johnson did, however, continue writing poems, patterning many of them after the work of the African-American poet Laurence Dunbar, who wrote in dialect.

Paul Laurence Dunbar

Paul Laurence Dunbar was one of the first African-American writers to become nationally known. Born in Dayton, Ohio (June 27, 1872), Dunbar's parents separated when he was around three years old. Dunbar was the only African-American at Central High School in Dayton, where he was editor of the school newspaper and class president. He started writing poetry early in life; his first poem was written when he was six and he gave his first public recitation when he was nine. In 1888, before Dunbar graduated from high school, the Dayton *Herald* newspaper published his first poems, "Our Martyred Soldiers" and "On The River."

Dunbar became friends with Wilbur and Orville Wright and edited a newspaper they owned, *The Tattler*. The United Brethren Publishing House published Dunbar's first collection of poetry, *Oak and Ivy*, in 1893. Durbar's second book, *Majors and Minors*, received an enthusiastic review from novelist and critic William Dean Howells in 1896, which led to Dunbar's work receiving national attention. Howells also wrote the introduction to Dunbar's *Lyrics of Lowly Life*, which combined his first two books into one volume.

Dunbar's poems and essays were published in a number of leading periodicals and in 1897 he gave a series of readings in London. That same year Dunbar obtained a job with the Library of Congress in Washington but soon left to concentrate on his writing and public readings. Here is a sample of the dialect poetry of Dunbar from his poem, "An Ante-Bellum Sermon."

An' yo' enemies may 'sail you
In de back an' in de front;
But de Lawd is all aroun' you,
Fu' to ba' de battle's brunt.
Dey kin fo'ge yo' chains an' shackles
F'om de mountains to de sea;
But de Lawd will sen' some Moses
Fu' to set his chillun free.

An' de lan' shall hyeah his thundah,
Lak a blas' f'om Gab'el's ho'n,
Fu' de Lawd of hosts is mighty
When he girds his ahmor on.
But fu' feah some one mistakes me,
I will pause right hyeah to say,
Dat I'm still a-preachin' ancient,
I ain't talkin' 'bout to-day.
But I tell you, fellah christuns,
Things'll happen mighty strange;
Now, de Lawd done dis fu' Isrul,
An' his ways don't nevah change,
An, de love he showed to Isrul
Wasn't all on Isrul spent;
Now don't run an' tell yo' mastahs
Dat I's preachin' discontent.

'Cause I isn't; I'se a-judgin'
Bible people by deir ac's;
I'se a-givin' you de Scriptuah,
I'se a-handin' you de fac's.
Cose ole Pher'oh b'lieved in slav'ry,
But de Lawd he let him see,
Dat de people he put bref in,
Evah mothah's son was free.

During the Spring of 1901 Johnson invited Dunbar, who he had seen in New York during the Johnson's first summer there (they had met previously) to come to Jacksonville for a public reading. The reading was successful; a large number of whites attended and Dunbar was a captivating speaker.

Dunbar remained in Jacksonville for about six weeks, staying with the Johnsons and Dunbar and James Johnson talked at length about dialect poetry. Later, Johnson realized that the "essential of traditional dialect poetry-the painting of humorous, contented, or forlorn 'darkies' in standardized colors against a conventional Arcadian background of log cabins and cotton fields—is itself a smooth-worn stereotype."[20]

An epiphany concerning Dunbar and "Negro dialect" came to Johnson after the poet's visit when he realized "the artificiality of conventionalized Negro dialect poetry; of its exaggerated geniality, childish optimism, forced comicality, and mawkish sentiment; of its limitation as an instrument of expression to but two emotions, pathos and humor, thereby making every poem either only sad or only funny."

"I could see that the poet writing in the conventionalized dialect, no matter how sincere he might be, was dominated by his audience," continued Johnson. "That his audience was a section of the white American reading public; that when he wrote he was expressing what often bore little relation, sometimes no relation at all, to actual Negro life; that he was really expressing only certain conceptions about Negro life that his audience was willing to accept and ready to enjoy; that, in fact, he wrote mainly for the delectation of an audience that was an outside group."[21]

In the Johnson's books on *Negro Spirituals*, published in 1925 and 1926, James Weldon Johnson states, "Negro dialect in America is the result of the effort of the slave to establish a medium of communication between himself and his master. This he did by dropping his original language, and formulating a phonologically and grammatically simplified English; that is, an English in which the harsh and difficult sounds were elided, and the secondary moods and tenses were eliminated. This dialect served not only as a means of communication between slave and master but also between slave and slave; so the original African languages became absolutely lost."[22]

Johnson noted that white Southerners readily understood Negro dialect because their own dialect was not markedly different. However, "Negro dialect is for many people made unintelligible on the printed page by the absurd practice of devising a clumsy, outlandish, so-called phonetic spelling for words in a dialect story or poem when the regular English spelling represents the very same sound. Paul Laurence Dunbar did a great deal to reform the writing down of dialect, but since it is more a matter of ear than of rules those who are not intimately familiar with the sounds continue to make the same blunders."[23]

Back to New York

At the end of May, 1901, Stanton was closed but Rosamond was still involved with his music students at the Baptist Academy when a fire started in La Villa, the area in Jacksonville where African-Americans lived. The fire destroyed Stanton. Shortly after this, the Johnsons returned to New York and arranged for a benefit concert for Stanton, which raised almost $1,000. Plans were soon made to rebuild the school and have it re-open in October; meanwhile, the Johnsons found that important changes had taken place during their time away from New York.

On West 53rd Street, between Sixth and Seventh Avenues, Negro proprietors had converted two private houses into hotels. The Johnsons moved into The Marshall, the hotel opened by Jimmy Marshall. The two hotels catered to the African-American community; they were fashionable, with good food and hosted a four-piece orchestra with dinner on Sunday nights.

The Marshall Hotel put the Johnsons in the midst of an elite African-American community of talented performers and show business professionals. They could live comfortably within this community and not have to seek meals or companionship at restaurants or hotels that might refuse them service. The Johnsons moved into a large back room on the second floor of the Marshall, installed a piano, and began writing songs.

Bob Cole lived nearby—two doors down from the Marshall—which was convenient for the trio working as a team. The group established a schedule. "We rose between nine and ten o'clock, breakfasted at about eleven, and began work not later than twelve," remembered Johnson. "When we didn't go to the theater, our working period approximated ten hours a day. We spent the time in actual writing or in planning future work." In late afternoon, they ate lunch in their room then, at midnight, went downstairs for supper, which sometimes "consisted of planked steak or broiled lobster. This supper generally cost us more than we were justified in spending; but, if we had done a good day's work, the money spent seemed a minor matter; if we hadn't made much progress, the gay air of the dining room, gayer around midnight than at any other hour, stimulated us."

On many evenings, Harry T. Burleigh, Will Marion Cook, Theodore Drury, Jack Nail and/or Paul Laurence Dunbar came by. There were discussions about "the manner and means of raising the status of the Negro as a writer, composer, and performer in the New York theater and world of music" with this group, remembered Johnson.

"The opinions advanced and maintained, often with more force than considerateness, were as diversified as the personalities in the group," he noted. "Cole was the most versatile man in the group and a true artist. In everything he did he strove for the fine artistic effect, regardless of whether it had any direct relation to the Negro or not. Nevertheless, there was an element of pro-Negro propaganda in all his efforts; and it showed, I think, most plainly when he was engaged in matching the white artist on the latter's own field."

Will Marion Cook "was the most original genius among all the Negro musicians," continued Johnson. "He had received excellent training in music, both in this country and in Berlin at the Hochschule; he had studied the violin under Joachim. But he had thrown all these standards over; he believed that the Negro in music and on the stage ought to be a Negro, a genuine Negro; he declared that the Negro should eschew 'White' patterns, and not employ his efforts in doing what 'the white artist could always do as well, generally better.'"[24]

Harry Burleigh "had been a student at the National Conservatory while Dvorak was the director," noted Johnson. "Not only had he studied with Dvorak but he had spent considerable time with him at his home. It was he who called the attention of the great Bohemian composer to the Negro spirituals."

"In all of our discussions and wrangles we were unanimous on one point; namely, that the managers, none of whom at that time could conceive of a Negro company playing anything but second and third-class theaters, had to be convinced" that a black musical could be successful in a first class theatre, stated Johnson.[25]

Will Marion Cook was working on a musical, *The Cannibal King*, and wanted Dunbar, who had worked with Cook on *Clorindy, or, The Origin of the Cakewalk* and *Jes Lak White Folks*, to work with him but Dunbar refused; the two did not get along. With Dunbar out of the picture, Johnson wrote the lyrics and Cole wrote the book for *The Cannibal King*. The musical was staged but was not successful; however, it later evolved into *In Dahomey*, starring Bert Williams and George Walker during the 1902-1903 season.

May Irwin was working on a new play, *The Belle of Bridgeport*, and Cole and the Johnson brothers were commissioned to write songs for it. In addition, they wrote songs for *Champagne Charlie*, a play by Peter Dailey, and *The Supper Club*, a two-act musical comedy produced by the Sire Brothers.

Marc Klaw and Abraham Erlanger were the dominant theatrical producers in New York in the early 1900s. Their firm, Klaw and Erlanger, "had more theatrical real estate, more money, and more power than anyone else in the business," according to David Jasen and Gene Jones in their book, *Spreadin' Rhythm Around*. Klaw was described as "the icy but mild-mannered financial overseer of their complicated enterprises" while Erlanger "was a crude, explosive tyrant who fancied himself the artistic arbiter of everything that went into the houses throughout their far-flung empire." As powerful members of the Theatrical Syndicate, an association of producers and landlords who controlled almost every major theatre in the country, "Klaw and Erlanger held a stranglehold on the American theatre. To a very great extent, they determined what got produced, and when and how it appeared, how long it stayed, and when and where it toured."[26]

A Drury Lane musical in London, *The Sleeping Beauty and the Beast*, had proven itself successful so Klaw and Erlanger imported it but wanted the show "Americanized" and, impressed with the Johnsons' song, "Run, Brudder Possum, Run," enlisted the team of Cole and the Johnson Brothers to write songs for the musical. Cole and the Johnsons wrote "Nobody's Lookin' But de Owl and de Moon," "Tell Me, Dusky Maiden" and "Come Out, Dinah, on the Green."

After this show, Johnson noted the trio "suddenly found ourselves programmed with 'top-notchers' among the writers of musical comedy."[27]

That same summer—1901—the team wrote "The Maiden with the Dreamy Eyes" for Anna Held in her play, *The Little Duchess*. This became another major hit song for them.

In August, 1901, Cole and the Johnsons took fifteen songs to the music publishing firm Joseph W. Stern and Company at 34 East 21st Street in New York. The songwriting team had already placed the songs in productions scheduled for the 1901-1902 season and the publisher signed them to a three-year contract. The writers were guaranteed a monthly income, which would be deducted from their semi-annual royalty payments.

The monthly draw was the songwriters' only income, so they were always short of cash. Bob Cole decided to not do a vaudeville tour that fall or winter—the first time he had not toured in ten years. Rosamond made up his mind that he was going to remain in New York as a composer but James Weldon was caught in a dilemma. The Stanton school was being rebuilt in Jacksonville during their time in New York and he was torn between staying in New York or returning to Florida. If Johnson gave up his job as principal of Stanton there was no turning back, and that job was a solid and prestigious job in the black community.

Stanton was scheduled to open in October but construction ran behind schedule; instead it opened during the first week of February, which gave Johnson a little more time to stay in New York. Cole and the Johnson brothers had songs in two shows; *The Sleeping Beauty* was set to open in November and *The Supper Club* would open in December.

Bob Cole and Rosamond Johnson had been contracted to entertain at a party a few days before James Weldon was scheduled to return to Jacksonville. The performance—which consisted of Cole and Johnson brothers songs—was a huge success and at the party were stars such as Lillian Russell and Edna Wallace Hooper as well as influential people from the theatre world. It was the beginning of Bob Cole and Rosamond Johnson's performing career as a duo.

Jacksonville: The Final Parting

James Weldon Johnson went back to his job at Stanton and mostly ignored his law practice because "I no longer had sufficient interest in it." Without Rosamond around, Johnson had little incentive to write. Instead, he concentrated on teaching and began to feel that his future lay in education. During the next summer an examination was scheduled which, if he passed, provided a life certificate in that profession; Johnson was determined to study for that test and pass it, which would establish a life-long career for him as a teacher.

The Johnson brothers corresponded regularly and one letter from Rosamond let Jim know that Bob Cole and Rosamond had impressed a theatre manager during the party held just before James left with the result that the duo was scheduled to appear on vaudeville stages for $300 a week. Since James would not be part of their act, he continued to study for the exam although, as May turned into June, he kept thinking about New York, the theatre world and the interesting group that congregated at the Marshall Hotel.

Johnson was studying for his teacher's examination on a hot afternoon in Jacksonville when two letters arrived from Rosamond. Stretched out in a hammock, Johnson looked at the postmarks on the letters and saw that both had been mailed at the same time, but one was lighter than the other. Johnson decided to open the lighter envelope first and saw it contained a short note from Rosamond and a money order for a little over $80 from song royalties. When he opened the second envelope, Johnson found a long letter from Rosamond and a money order for $400 from more royalties.

During the first half of 1902 their songs had sold enough sheet music to pay back their publishers the money advanced and net almost $1,500! Their biggest seller was "The Maiden With the Dreamy Eyes" but other songs were selling too. Johnson looked at the checks and the letter and asked himself "Why in the world was I hanging on down in Jacksonville?"[28]

When James Weldon Johnson arrived back in New York he was

surprised to find that his brother and Bob Cole had become quite fashionable; their clothes were expensive, and they each owned a dozen pair of shoes and a number of shirts, ties and socks. They assured him they needed those clothes for their act. They had expanded their living quarters as well; James and Rosamond lived in two back rooms of the Marshall but Cole had moved into the Marshall and he and Rosamond added front and middle rooms that connected with the back rooms. The back room became their "work room" where they wrote songs.

The Cole and Johnson duo was headlining at Keith's 14th Street Theatre, a major vaudeville house. In their act, Cole and Johnson wore evening clothes and their show opened with them discussing a party where they were scheduled to entertain. Rosamond sat at the piano and played Paderewski's "Minuet," then suggested they follow with a short classical song and sang "Still wie die Nacht" in German. Cole then commented that classical music might not find favor with those at the party and suggested they sing some of the songs they had written. From this point forward, the act consisted of Cole and Johnson performing original songs; it was a huge success.

At the hotel, the trio worked on songs, although James often worked alone because Cole and Rosamond performed two shows each day. The duo was scheduled to play the Orpheum Circuit during that winter, which meant going to the West Coast and back, so the group sometimes wrote early in the morning and again late at night. One of the first songs they wrote was "Under the Bamboo Tree" and they played it for Marie Cahill, who was starring in a musical, *Sally In Our Alley*. She was soon performing "Under the Bamboo Tree" in her show and her performances introduced the song, which became a worldwide popular hit. (It was revived in the 1944 film, *Meet Me in St. Louis*, starring Judy Garland.)

As Fall approached, James was faced with the dilemma of whether to remain in New York, writing songs, or leave for Jacksonville and resume his role as principal of Stanton. Johnson was torn with that decision. He noted that, as songwriters, they were not earning enough money to live on, although Cole and Rosamond earned a nice income performing in vaudeville; however, he refused to take part of that income for himself. He debated going back to Jacksonville until the next summer, when he planned to return and re-join the group. His friends in Jacksonville were stunned that he would even consider leaving such a prominent, solid position as school principal.

Johnson could not make up his mind but finally wrote a letter resigning his position at Stanton. During the next day the letter stayed in his pocket then, that night as the three songwriters walked up Broadway, he dropped the letter into a mail box.

"As the letter dropped into the box, a load dropped from my shoulders," said Johnson. "I at once became aware of an expanse of freedom I had not felt before. Immediately it seemed that the goal of my efforts was no longer marked by a limit just a little way in front of my eyes but reached out somewhere toward infinity. From the thought that the things I had already done, I had done, perhaps, fairly well, I got a solid satisfaction; but stepping off my beaten road on to a path that led I knew not just where gave me a thrill."[29]

Cole and Johnson were scheduled to begin their West Coast tour in early 1902 so a few days before their scheduled departure the trio went to their music publishers for their royalty check, which was based on the sales of sheet music. The check was for $6,000. In July, their check for the first six months of 1902 was over $12,000. By this time, their list of money-making hits included "The Maiden with the Dreamy Eyes," "Man, Won't You Let Me Be Your Beau,'" "Nobody's Lookin' But de Owl and de Moon," "Tell Me, Dusky Maiden," "The Old Flag Never Touched the Ground," "My Castle on the Nile," "Under the Bamboo Tree," and "Oh, Didn't He Ramble." "The Congo Love Song," a new song written for Marie Cahill, also became a major hit for them.

Alone in New York while Rosamond and Bob Cole were on tour, James Weldon Johnson worked on ideas for new songs, attended a number of theatrical productions, including those at the Metropolitan Opera, and read a good deal. Since he found himself with plenty of spare time he decided to enroll at Columbia University, where he studied English and the history and development of the theatre under Professor Brander Matthews.

After their return, Cole and the Johnson Brothers worked on *Humpty Dumpty*, a Drury Lane musical that Klaw and Erlanger had brought over from London and wanted "Americanized." This was the first play produced in the new New Amsterdam Theater, top of the line with New York Theaters, and Cole and the Johnson brothers wrote the songs. Their song, "Fishing" was sung by Fay Templeton.

Politics

During the summer of 1904, James Weldon Johnson was invited by Charles W. Anderson to join the "Colored Republican Club" on West 53rd street. The club, located across the street from the Marshall Hotel, was furnished nicely and Anderson wanted Johnson to be "Chairman" of the House Committee, which meant Johnson managed the money and facility. Johnson recruited some of the talent who hung around the Marshall for an "entertainment night" once a week and these soon became popular gatherings.

This was James Weldon Johnson's introduction to Republican politics and it came through a confidant of Booker T. Washington, the most prominent black man in America and the spokesman for the race. Washington had a close, strong connection to President Teddy Roosevelt. Roosevelt had invited Washington to dine with him at the White House and later met with Washington in Washington's home on the Tuskegee campus in Alabama, which caused a backlash with Roosevelt's Southern followers. Washington recommended black candidates for federal offices which Roosevelt often appointed during his terms in office.

Booker T. Washington received national recognition in 1895 from his speech at the Cotton States Exposition held in Atlanta. In the "Atlanta Speech" Washington addressed the concerns of whites towards integration, stating, "in all things that are purely social we can be as separate as the fingers, yet one as the hand in all things essential to mutual progress." Washington "went on to say that agitation for social equality was folly and to call for blacks to seek industrial skills as the means to economic improvement."[30]

The speech came at an opportune time for Washington because Frederick Douglass, who had long been the nationally recognized spokesman for black Americans, had died the year before. The death of Douglass, and the rise of Washington, created another movement, led by W.E.B. DuBois, who vied to become the spokesman for black America. The conflict between these two men—and two movements—continued until Washington's death.

Timothy Fortune, editor of the New York *Age*, was a close confidant and advisor to Washington but the two argued after Fortune published an editorial criticizing a speech Washington made. This led Washington to turn to Charles Anderson as his principal advisor in Republican politics. During the 1904 Republican Convention in Chicago, Washington told Anderson to inform the 1,000 black delegates what Roosevelt had done for African-Americans; Anderson did so and blacks supported Roosevelt in the 1904 election.

During the 1904 election, the Johnson brothers and Bob Cole wrote a campaign song for President Teddy Roosevelt's election, "You're All Right, Teddy." The most popular tune during Roosevelt's campaign was the ragtime song "A Hot Town in the Cold Town Tonight," to which supporters penned campaign lyrics.

After Roosevelt was elected, Anderson was appointed Collector of Internal Revenue for a district in New York and James Weldon Johnson became president of the Colored Republican Club.

A Theatrical Production Company

The songwriting trio continued to write songs during the winter of 1904-1905. Their song, "Lazy Moon" became popular and Cole and Johnson remained a popular vaudeville act, playing the top theaters, but Cole had bigger ambitions.

Bob Cole wanted to drop out of vaudeville so he and the Johnsons could form a theatrical company and stage musicals. Cole felt they could net $30,000-40,000 a year with their own theater company and, if that failed, he and Rosamond could always return to vaudeville. Rosamond liked the idea but James countered—rather strongly—that, as songwriters and vaudeville performers, they were not burdened by the worries and responsibilities of a large troupe so they could concentrate on their writing.

James had another reason to oppose Cole's idea; he knew that Cole saw him as the business manager for the company "and I had no desire to go trouping around the country and undergoing the hardships that every colored company had to put up with; nor did I have any intention of doing so, if there was any way to avoid it."[31]

Early in 1905, Cole and Johnson were booked on the Orpheum Circuit so the trio went to the West Coast for a string of performances. When they returned to New York, the vaudeville team discovered they were scheduled to appear at the Palace Theater in London for six weeks. The group decided to spend three months in Europe, starting in Paris, then go through Belgium and Holland before they landed in London. In Paris, the group heard an orchestra perform two of their songs, "Under the Bamboo Tree" and "The Congo Love Song."

Back in New York, Johnson found his enthusiasm for the theater and songwriting waning; he wanted to do "literary work," which meant books and poetry and he wanted to finish his studies at Columbia. He had to "spur" himself to write songs because "Being light enough for Broadway was beginning to be, it seemed, a somewhat heavy task. Unconscious of what was taking place I was actually making a mental shift and adjustment."[32]

Cole and Johnson were booked for a return engagement to London that Spring and Cole wanted these to be their final vaudeville performances and then return to the United States in the Fall and develop their own show. Cole had already sketched out a play, to be called *The Shoo-Fly Regiment.*

The trio began writing the show and, before Cole and Johnson left for London, James Weldon Johnson had written lyrics and helped Cole with the dialogue while Rosamond had composed most of the music. As they worked, James "experienced strange emotions while doing my part in creating *The Shoo-Fly Regiment,* for I felt that it was the last piece of work the three of us should do together."[33]

During the time they worked on the play, Charles Anderson approached Johnson about going into the Diplomatic Service. Johnson agreed that, if appointed by the President, he would go.

"Arriving at this decision was not an easy matter; not nearly so easy as the decision to leave Jacksonville," said Johnson. "New York had been a good godmother to me, almost a fairy godmother, and it gave me a wrench to turn my back on her. Over against all that life and work in New York meant, I balanced three things, and they tipped the scales. I put into the scales my desire to avoid the disagreeable business of traveling round the country under the conditions that a Negro theatrical company had to endure; as I proposed to cite, among my qualifications for the Service, Spanish as a foreign language, I expected to be appointed to a South American post, so there was added the allure of the adventure of life on a strange continent; but heavier than either of these was the realization, which came upon me suddenly, that time was slipping and I had not yet made a real start on the work that I had long kept reassuring myself I should sometime do, that the opportunity for seizing that 'Sometime' had come, and that I ought not let it pass. Then, the feeling came over me that, in leaving New York, I was not making a sacrifice, but an escape; that I was getting away, if only for a while, from the feverish flutter of life to seek a little stillness of the spirit."[34]

Johnson told Rosamond and Cole of his plans and they accepted them, reasoning that he could always come back to New York and the adventure might present some new ideas for comic operas.

As Spring, 1906 ended, Bob Cole and Rosamond Johnson sailed to London for their return engagement while James Weldon Johnson sailed for Venezuela, where he would be consul. James Weldon Johnson was in Venezuela when *The Shoo-Fly Regiment* gave its first performance in August, 1906 in Washington, D.C.

The Shoo-Fly Regiment

The Shoo-Fly Regiment was a three act comedy set during the time of the Spanish-American War. The first and third acts were set in Alabama at an industrial school (modeled on Tuskegee Institute) and the second act was set in Manila, the Philippines. The plot involved a young graduate of the school who joins the armed service for the War.

Military themes were popular for musicals; there was plenty of action on stage and national pride was captured in patriotic songs. *The Shoo-Fly Regiment* capitalized on this with a twist: they presented black soldiers in their musical. *The Shoo-Fly Regiment* also broke the taboo against having serious love scenes in black shows.

James Reese Europe

When they began work on *The Shoo Fly Regiment*, the Johnsons and Cole began working with African-American bandleader James Reese Europe.

Europe was born in Mobile, Alabama on February 22, 1880 and his family moved to Washington, D.C. in 1889; two years later, the Europe family moved into a home just a few doors down from the home of John Philip Sousa, the popular bandleader and composer of marches such as "Stars and Stripes Forever" and "The Washington Post March." Sousa led one of the most popular brass bands in America during a time when brass bands enjoyed their greatest popularity; it was estimated that there were 150,000 bandsmen playing in 10,000 brass bands during this time.[35]

In late 1902 or early 1903, James Reese Europe moved to New York City, then seen as the center for African-American entertainers and performers, where he joined his brother, John Europe, who performed at the Little Savoy, owned by Barron Wilkins on West 35th Street.[36]

Europe served as the director of the orchestra and chorus for *A Trip To Africa* in 1904; this initiated his career in black music theater. During the Fall of 1904, he had some of his songs published by Sol Bloom; the most successful of these was "Blue Eyed Sue."

During the late winter of 1905, as Bob Cole and the Johnson brothers were writing *The Shoo-Fly Regiment,* they formed a strong cast, with Cole and J. Rosamond Johnson starring, supported by Tom Brown, Sam Lucan, Theodore Pankey, and Anna Cook. James Reese Europe was asked to direct the orchestra and the forty-member chorus.[38] The cast for *The Shoo-fly Regiment* rehearsed for a month, then began a tour before it played in New York.

James Europe and James Weldon Johnson had written "What It Takes to Make Me Love You, You've Got It," with Johnson supplying the lyrics to Europe's melody, before production of *The Shoo-Fly Regiment*.

Songs listed in the program for *The Shoo-Fly Regiment* included "The Bo'd of Education," "On The Gay Luneta" and "The Old Flag Never Touched the Ground," which all credited James Weldon Johnson (Europe is credited on "On the Gay Luneta"). Other songs in the musical were "Sugar Babe," "I Can't Think of Nothing in the Wide, Wide World But You," "Once Upon a Time," "There's Always Something Wrong," "Who Do You Love?," "Won't You Be My Little Brown Bear?," "My Susanna," "I'll Fight (for the Dear Old Flag)," "Li'l Gal," "Just How Much I Love You," and "Floating Down the Nile."

There were sixty members in the company when they began their tour but Cole and Rosamond Johnson faced difficulties playing short-term engagements in second class theaters with long miles in between. Financing the show depended on them and, in early 1907, they had to lay off members when they ran out of money. *The Shoo-Fly Regiment* opened at the Grand Opera House on Broadway in New York on June 3, 1907 but soon closed because Cole and Johnson could not meet the payroll. They reopened at the Bijou Theater in August but only ran for two weeks; however, the exposure allowed them to spend a second season on the road. This time out Cole and Johnson were more successful.[37]

Jim Europe left *The Shoo-Fly Regiment* in March and joined S.H. Dudley and the Smart Set Company, then joined *The Black Politician*, which debuted in September, 1908, before he re-joined Cole and Johnson in preparation of their new production *The Red Moon* for the 1908 Fall season.[38]

The Red Moon

Cole and Johnson had begun work on *The Red Moon*, subtitled *An American Musical in Red and Black,* after the second tour of *The Shoo-fly Regiment*. The plot involves Minnehaha, a half-Indian, half-black woman who is kidnapped from her home in Virginia to re-join her tribe. Bob Cole played "Plunk Green" (Minnehaha's boyfriend) and J. Rosamond Johnson played "Slim Brown" and the two set out to find her. They did find her and she was returned to her home after a series of adventures that had Cole and Johnson impersonating a doctor and lawyer with clever flim flam.

The Red Moon was the most ambitious, the most successful, and the last of Cole and Johnson's full-length musical comedy productions. Songs in *The Red Moon* included "Big Red Shawl," "Last of the Setting Sun," "I Want to Be an Indian," "I Ain't Had No Lovin' in a Long Time (an' Lovin' is a Thing I Need)" (lyrics by Cole and music by Europe), "Sambo" (lyrics by Cole) "Ada, My Sweet Potater" (Europe and Cole wrote the music – Charles Hunter did lyrics).[39] "Roll Them Cotton Bales," written by James Weldon Johnson and Rosamond, was the original opening chorus for *The Red Moon*.

During the tour of *The Red Moon* Cole and Johnson once again had trouble meeting the payroll. In December James Europe and Abbie Mitchell left the show. By the spring of 1910, the show's creators were tired and nearly broke.

According to Jasen and Jones, *The Red Moon* "is Cole and Johnson's best score, a fresh amalgam of Indian music, Tin Pan Alley syncopation, ballads, and dialect numbers." Ed Marks called *The Red Moon* "The most tuneful colored show of the century." Jasen and Jones noted further that "Eubie Blake was still playing "Bleeding Moon" sixty years after he first heard it."[40]

When *The Red Moon* closed, Cole and Johnson announced they would not produce a show for the upcoming season because large shows could not make money in "popular priced" (read: second-class) theatres. They were going back to vaudeville as a duo. In October 1910 they were at Keith's Fifth Avenue Theatre, leading the bill at $750 a week."[41]

Bob Cole collapsed on stage on the last night of their engagement at Keith's; he was suffering both mental and physical distress. Taken first to Bellevue Hospital, he was then moved to Manhattan State Hospital for several months. Tests at private clinics labeled his diagnosis as a nervous breakdown. Needing rest, but separated from his wife Stella, his mother, Isabella Cole came and arranged for his recuperation at a boarding house in the Catskills. After several quiet days spent sitting on the porch and swimming, he seemed to be improving. However, while swimming with friends a few days later, he suddenly went still and disappeared under the water. His death by drowning, on August 2, 1911, was probably a suicide."[42]

The 1908-1909 season was, in many ways, a very good one for black musical theater. *The Red Moon* had a successful year, although they were still plagued by financial problems. Still, Cole, Johnson and Europe planned to take the show on the road again that fall. Williams and Walker, the other major African-American company, closed the second year of their well-received production *Bandanna Land* (book and lyrics by Jesse Shipp and Alex Rogers, music by Will Marion Cook) at the Yorkville Theatre in Brooklyn in April after playing Broadway. This was the first black show to play at the Belasco Theatre in Washington, D.C., which was previously a white-only theatre. However, George Walker became too ill to continue in February so his wife, Aida Overton Walker, took over his part for the last two months. Those performances were George Walker's last stage appearances. In May, Ernest Hogan died; on January 8, 1911, Walker died.

The loss of Ernest Hogan, George Walker and Bob Cole within a two year period was devastating to black theatre; it marked the end of the first black Broadway era.

Johnson Returns to New York

James Weldon Johnson served as Consul in Venezuela, then moved on to Nicaragua; during his time in Central and South America he married Grace Nail, sister of John Nail. Johnson's tenure in the diplomatic corps ended with the election of President Woodrow Wilson in 1912; after taking office in 1913, Wilson replaced Republican appointees with his own Democratic appointments.

James Weldon Johnson returned to New York and wrote more songs with his brother, including "When It's All Going Out and Nothing's Coming In." According to Rosamond Johnson, this was the last song that he and his brother wrote together, although he continued to put James Weldon's poems to music.

In their book, *Spreadin' Rhythm Around: Black Popular Songwriters, 1880-1930,* authors David Jasen and Gene Jones ignore the contributions of James Weldon Johnson when they state, "The most successful black musical theatre writers of the early century were the prolific Bob Cole and J. Rosamond Johnson. They delivered the goods—to producers, to publishers, to audiences, to actors—for ten years. Their songs were interpolated into nearly thirty Broadway shows, providing showstoppers for stars and hits for publication. In an age that expected charm in the theatre, they wrote to order. They moved faster and did more than their contemporaries because they carried less weight. Without the philosophical baggage of Cook, or the burden of stardom shouldered by Williams and Walker, they were freer to work, whenever and wherever occasions arose. Their commitment was to show business, not to ideology."[43]

The authors note, again dismissing James Weldon Johnson, that "Bob Cole was—with the possible exception of George M. Cohan—the most versatile theatre talent of his day. He was an actor, a librettist, a lyricist, a director, a singer, and dancer, and producer, and a composer" and that his name is on "nearly 120 song sheets as composer and/or lyricist, making him the most-published black writer of his era. Cole and his main partner, the composer J. Rosamond Johnson, were the only black writers of that time to have long-term relationships with a Broadway producer and with a major publisher. Each relationship fed the other: their theatre songs were likely to be published and their published songs were likely to be featured in shows. Cole and Johnson didn't make the rounds, nor did they wait in offices with librettos and lead sheets in hand. They were working pros; they were in demand."[44]

ASCAP

The American Society of Composers, Authors and Publishers (ASCAP), a performing rights organization, was formed at the Hotel Claridge in New York by songwriter and publisher Victor Herbert on February, 13, 1914. The organization was dedicated to protecting song copyrights and collecting monies for the public performances of songs. Among the founding members were Irving Berlin, Jerome Kern and John Philip Sousa. In March, James Weldon Johnson was elected to membership in that organization. His letter, sent by Glen MacDonough, stated, "It gives me much pleasure to inform you that at a recent meeting of the Board of Directors of the Society of American Composers, Authors and Publishers, you were elected a member. Your initiation fee and dues for the first year will jointly amount to ten dollars."[45] Thus James Weldon Johnson became one of the founding members of the first performing rights organization formed in the United States.

Conclusion

The Red Moon ended the songwriting collaborations of Cole and the Johnson Brothers. During the New York run of *The Red Moon*, J. Rosamond Johnson was approached by producer Ray Comstock to compose the score to *Mr. Lode of Koal*, Bert Williams' first solo show. Rosamond Johnson continued to perform in vaudeville, wrote music for a theater review in London, served as director of New York's Music School Settlement for Colored and formed his own ensembles, The Harlem Rounders and The Inimitable Five.

After James Weldon Johnson returned to New York on December 10, 1912, shortly after the election of President Woodrow Wilson, he sought to continue in the diplomatic service but was confronted with the facts that his political affiliation and race were two major strikes against him. On September 1, 1913, he submitted his letter of resignation to Wilson's Secretary of State, William Jennings Bryan, which was accepted a little over a week later.

During his six years in South and Central America he wrote a number of poems and completed his novel, *The Autobiography of an Ex-Colored Man*, which was published in mid-1912. Wanting to continue his literary career, Johnson turned down offers to return to Stanton as principal and to set up a law practice. He accepted a position as head of the editorial page at the black weekly, the *New York Age*. This eventually led to Johnson becoming the first black executive secretary of the NAACP.

Johnson's brother-in-law, John Nail, was a major developer of Harlem and played a leading role in that section of New York becoming the home for blacks and black businesses. Harlem became a vibrant center for black writers, actors and musicians and, during the 1920s when the Harlem Renaissance became the catch-all phrase for a flowering of African-American art, writing and theatre, James Weldon Johnson was well positioned to be a leading member of an elite Harlem community. It was during the Harlem Renaissance that black theatre was revived with musicals such as *Shuffle Along, Run-*

ning Wild and *Blackbirds* produced on Broadway. However, by this time Johnson was busy with his duties at the NAACP, although he continued to write books and articles-but not songs.

James Weldon Johnson

Lyrics

Ain't Dat Scan'lous (1901)

Words: Bob Cole and James Weldon Johnson
Music: Rosamond Johnson

Bad Land Bill done tho'w his shoe
Wid Miss Lucy Jane
Ever since he took her to de fancy ball
Soon as he got in de hall
Took his walkin' cane
Smashed de shiny beaver hat of Beebe Small
Beebe was de Beau Brummell
Of his social set
There-fo' had to show de crowd dat he was game
So he tackled Bad Land Bill,
'Twas fight you bet
Causing all de ladies to exclaim

Now ain't dat scan'lous!
For to act dat way!
Now ain't dat awful!
Well I should say!
To see such impropriety
Amongst de best society
Now ain't dat scan'lous!
Well I should say!

To another swell affair
Bill thought he would go
He was told dat only evening clothes were right
So he gathered all his change,
Went into a sto',
Asked to see some clothes to wear only at night

Bill then took de garments home,
Put them on with pride,
In a cab up to de hall then he was drawn,
Soon as he got in de do',
Every body cried,
When they saw he had pajamas on

An Explanation (1914)

Words: James Weldon Johnson
Music: Will Marion Cook.

Jedge pr-foun' settin' down
Tryin' Brudder Johnsing fer a-lib'lin' Brudder Brown
Solemn jury full o'dignity
Wid de pompous manner ob de ol' darkey
Jedge a-rose den he took a pose
An' thus he spake in tones dat rang
An' thrilled an' chilled an' froze:

"Noble breddren, mos' hones' men,
Br'er Brown will question Johnsing
ob de where-fores an' de when
Br'er Brown spoke brief:
"Look heah! 'Splain to me de reason Ho!
Way yo' said to Squire Lee
Dat dere was twelve ol' chicken stealers in-a dis town
Includin' me?

Brudder Johnsing ansyer'd:
"Ef he tol' yo' datt, my brudder
Why, he said sumpin' dat warn't true
Warn't true,
Kase what I said wuz dis:
Dat dere wuz twelve wifout includin' you!
I said, wifout includin' you-oooo-oo-oo"!

The Animals Convention (1902)

Words: James Weldon Johnson
Music: Rosamond Johnson

Once der was a meetin' in de wilderness
All de creatures of creation dey was dar
Brudder Rabbit, Brudder Possum, Brudder Wolf
Brudder Fox, King Lion
Mister Terrapin and Mister B'ar
De question for discussion was, "Who is de bigges' man?"
Dey 'pointed oler Jedge Owl to decide
So he polished up his spectacles, an' put 'em on his nose,
An' in dese words Jedge Owl he re-plied

Brudder Wolf am mighty cunnin'
Brudder Fox am mighty sly
Brudder Terrapin an' Possum kinder small
Brudder Lion mighty vicious,
Brudder B'ar he sorter 'speicious
Brudder Rabbit you'se de cutes' of them all

Dis caused a great confusion 'mongst de animals
Ev'ry creature claimed dat he had won de prize
Dey disputed, an dey arg'ed, an' dey growled,
An' dey roared,
An' den, pretty soon de dust began to rise.
Brer Rabbit he jes' stood aside,
An' urged 'em on to fight,
Brer Lion he mos' tore Brer B'ar in two;
An' when dey was all so ti-ahd
Dat dey couldn't catch der bref,
Brer Rabbit he jes grabbed de prize an' flew

The Awakening (1913)

Words: James Weldon Johnson
Music: J. Rosamond Johnson

I dreamt that I was a rose
That grew beside a lonely way
Close by a path none ever chose
And there I linger'd day by day
Beneath the sunshine and show'r
I grew and waited there apart
Gathering perfume hour by hour
And storing it within my heart
Yet never knew just why I waited there and grew

I dreamt that you were a bee
That one day gaily flew along
You came across the hedge to me
And sang a soft love burden'd song
You brushed my petals with a kiss
I woke to gladness with a start
And yielded up to you in bliss
The treasured fragrant of my heart
And then I knew that I had waited there for you

Carve Dat Possum

Words: James Weldon Johnson
Music: Bob Cole

When de leaves begin to fall,
And de frost is on de ground,
And de 'simmons is a-ripe-nin' on de tree
When I hear de dinner call
And de chillen gadders 'round
Oh! 'tis den de 'possum is de meat for me!

Carve dat 'possum,
Carve dat 'possum, chillen,
Carve dat 'possum,
Carve him to de heart

When de Winter days are past,
And de Spring has come at last,
When de good ole Summer sun begins to shine
Oh! My thoughts den take a turn,
And my heart begins to fall,
Makes it hard to tell which time of year am bes'
Watermelon, watermelon, chillen,
Watermelon growin' on de vine

Oh! De year will surely bring on a season for us all,
Ev'ry one kin pick his season f'om de res'
But de mellon in de Spring, and de 'possum in de Fall
Makes it hard to tell which time of year am bes'

Watermelon, and dat 'possum, chillen,
Watermelon, both am berry fine

Come Out, Dinah, On the Green (Darkey Serenade) (1901)

Words: Bob Cole and James Weldon Johnson
Music: Rosamond Johnson

Dinah dear, while all is still and sleeping,
And the moon above the hill is creeping,
Underneath your window, love, a-pining,
I sing a serenade to you,
Vowing by the stars above a-shining
That my love is true, oh, Dinah,
There's none diviner

Oh, Dinah, promise tonight you will be mine,
Ah! Dinah, underneath your window love, I'm singing
Don't you hear my merry banjo ringing?
Dinah, dear, lend your beauty to the scene
Dinah, round my heart like ivy you are clinging
Dinah, you're my queen, won't you come out?
Come out, come out,
Dinah on the green

Dinah dear, the soft south wind is sighing,
And the stars down through the trees are spying,
I am here your love to claim, believe me
You are my all, my heart's delight
If you do not take my name, 'twill grieve me,
Tell me yes, tonight, oh, Dinah,
There's no diviner

Oh, Dinah, promise tonight you will be mine,
Ah! Dinah, underneath your window love, I'm singing
Don't you hear my merry banjo ringing?
Dinah, dear, lend your beauty to the scene
Dinah, round my heart like ivy you are clinging
Dinah, you're my queen, won't you come out?
Come out, come out,
Dinah on the green

Como Le Gusta? (How Do You Like Me?) (1904)

Words: James Weldon Johnson
Music: Bob Cole

Now once there lived a very gay lothario
Who never failed to win at hearts wherever he'd go
And love had never caused his heart one moment of pain
Until he reached the Land of Sunny Spain
'Twas there he saw the Spanish maidens
With those fathomless eyes
They say behind a fan, "Win me, sir! If you can"
But when he summoned all his arts and wiles
To win one prize
Some other Spanish maiden just as fair would say

"Como le gusta, my eyes, Senor?
Como le gusta my smile?
Como le gusta my size, Senor?
Como le gusta my style?
Como le gusta my hair, Senor?
Look-a-me over, and see
Como le gusta me?
Como le gusta me?"

Then like a bee amid sweet roses wet with dew
Around and 'round not knowing where to light he flew
So many dark-eyed beauties dawn'd upon his sight
Until his heart was dizzy with delight
But when the gay lothario who thought himself so wise
Said: "now no time I'll lose, here's where I'll pick and choose"
Each pretty maid exclaimed: "How dare you? Sir!"
With flashing eyes and left him guessing
As she smiled and said again

"Como le gusta, my eyes, Senor?
Como le gusta my smile?
Como le gusta my size, Senor?
Como le gusta my style?
Como le gusta my hair, Senor?
Look-a-me over, and see
Como le gusta me?
Como le gusta me?"

Congo Love Song (1900)

Words: James Weldon Johnson
Music: Rosamond Johnson

'Way down where the Congo is a-flowing
'Way down where the bamboo is a-growing
Down where tropic breezes are a-blowing
There once lived a little Zulu maid
Each night very silently canoeing
Upstream came a Kafir chief a-wooing
He came for the maiden's hand a-suing
Singing as along the banks they strayed

CHORUS:
As long as the Congo flows to the sea
As long as a leaf grows on the bamboo tree
My love and devotion will be deep as the ocean
Won't you take a notion for to love-a but me?

Maiden though his gentle words believing
Told him that she thought he was deceiving
This set his poor Kafir heart a-grieving
Yet, he never changed his ardent theme
One night to her father's kraal he traced her
And there in his lusty arms embraced her
Then in his canoe he gently placed her
Singing as they floated down the stream

This maid in the wilds of Ombagooda
Down where this bold Kafir chieftain wooed her
May have been perhaps a trifle cruder
Than girls on the Hudson or the Seine
Yet though she was but a little Zulu
She did just what other artful maids do
And showed there were tricks of love that she knew
For she kept him singing this refrain

Cupid's Ramble or Cupid's Blind They Say (1908)

Words: Bob Cole and James Weldon Johnson
Music: Rosamond Johnson

CUPID: Cupid is out upon a ramble
And to his archery who knows
But you may fall a victim;
Cupid, you know is very clever,
Aren't you afraid?

GIRLS: Cupid I know is very sly
But on the rogue I have always kept a watchful eye;

CUPID: Yet some day you will fall by Cupid's knavery and bravery
GIRLS: His knavery and bravery
CUPID: To slavery
GIRLS: What! Slavery?

CUPID: Fate has issued this decree
GIRLS: What is it, Pray?
CUPID: That each maid his slave shall be
GIRLS: We dread the day
CUPID: I think such bondage you will welcome
GIRLS: Will you tell me, how could that be?

CUPID: Listen now! I'll tell you how
And his slave you'll be, I vow
GIRLS: Not if I can help it, Sir!
To be free I would prefer

CUPID: Bear in mind! A lord more kind,
To serve fair maid you'll never find;
GIRLS: That does not assure me
That does not allure me

CUPID: I shall stand enraptured
Maiden when you're captured

GIRLS: By this I surmise you are Cupid in disguise
And of you I must beware

CHORUS:
CUPID: "Cupid's blind," they say
GIRLS: The reckless rambler
CUPID: But when he shoots his dart
You will find it never goes astray
GIRL: In hearts a gambler,
BOTH: You will find it never goes astray
But always strikes somebody's heart

GIRLS: Cupid I've heard is very cunning
But any careful maid, I'm sure
Would have no cause to fear him;
Although I know he's very artful
I'm not afraid

CUPID: Don't be too sure my pretty maid;
For he has upset the best of plans that ever were laid
GIRLS: I watch him tho' he moves about suspiciously,
CUPID: Suspiciously
GIRLS: Capriciously
CUPID: Capriciously
GIRLS: Judiciously
CUPID: Judiciously
Even though he'll baffle you

GIRLS: You think it so?
What then should a maiden do?
We'd like to know
CUPID: I vow that

He will never harm you
GIRLS: Should that be, Sir! I'll agree Sir!
Every heart by Cupid's art
Must be pinioned with his dart
Tell me, Sir! You're so expert,
Should he hit me, would it hurt?
CUPID: Fear no ills, no blood he spills
Although he wounds he seldom kills
GIRLS: May good fortune send me
Someone to defend me
I shall stand enraptured
CUPID: Maiden when you're captured
GIRLS: By this I surmise
You are Cupid in disguise
And of you I must beware
CUPID: Cupid's blind" they say
GIRLS: The reckless rambler
CUPID: But when he shoots his dart
GIRLS: In hearts a gambler
BOTH: You will find it never goes away
But always strikes somebody's heart

De Bo'd Of Education (1906)

Words: James Weldon Johnson
Music: J. Rosamond Johnson

A man kin study hard in books,
And grad-u-ate from school
And yet dat man kin be wid ease
De biggest kind of fool
But how kin any man wid brains
Deny de allegation
Dat it takes lots o sense for a pusson to be
On de Bo'd of Education

We is de Bo'd
We is de Bo'd
De Bo'd of Education
We is de men dat su-pren-ten'
Each school examination
Answers dat we can't cri-tick-size
We let dem pass
An' jes' look wise
We is de Bo'd
We is de Bo'd,
De Bo'd of Education

Dey teaches child-un now in school
Some things we never heard
We cant dispute dere arguments
And so we take dere word
Dat sunshine comes a billion miles
Be-fo' we all receive it
Might be true in December but 'long in July
Der's nobody would believe it
Dey tell us dat de earth ain't flat

And dat de sun don't move
Now dat's an easy thing to say
But mighty hard to prove
For Josh-way told de sun to stop
And it don't need no provin'
Dat he would not ha' spoken to de sun that way
If de sun had not been movin'

Dey say de earth goes spinnin' round
'Heap faster than a top
And dat we all should tumble off
If it should ever stop
Dey call dat science, well we know,
'Tain't common sense, Doggone it!
And de bes' kind o' proof dat it don't spin around
Is de fact we all stay on it

De Little Pickaninny's Gone to Sleep (1910)

Words: James Weldon Johnson
Music: J. Rosamond Johnson

Cuddle down, ma honey, in yo' bed
Go to sleep and rest yo' little head
Been a kind o' ailin' all de day
Didn't have no spirit for to play
Never mind, tomorrow it's a fack
Daddy's gwine to ride you on his back
Round and round de cabin flo' so fast
Der! He's closed his little eyes at last

De little pickaninny's gone to sleep
Cuddled in his trundle bed so tiny
De little pickaninny's gone to sleep
Closed his little eyes so bright and shiny
Hush! And when you walk across de flo'
Step across it very soft and slow
De shadows all around begin to creep
De little pickaninny's gone to sleep

Mandy, what's de matter wid dat chile?
Keeps a sighin' every little while
Seems to me I heard him kinder groan
Lord! His little hands am cold as stone!
What's dat far off light dat's in his eyes
Dat's de light dat shines from out de skies
Fold his little hands across his breast
Let de little pickaninny rest

De little pickaninny's gone to sleep
Cuddled in his trundle bed so tiny
De little pickaninny's gone to sleep
Closed his little eyes so bright and shiny
Hush! And when you walk across de flo'
Step across it very soft and slow
De shadows all around begin to creep
De little pickaninny's gone to sleep

Dem Lovin' Words Sound Mighty Good to Me (1905)

Words: James Weldon Johnson
Music: Rosamond Johnson

Mose Jenkins who had been to school,
And learned to read a book,
Went out one night to see his gal,
And 'long with him he took,
A bunch of fancy loving talk,
And words that he had read,
And as soon as he got in the house,
He took her hand and said,
"You am de darlin' of ma dreams,
De sunlight of ma skies,
Ma star of hope, ma hearts desire
You am ma precious prize"
She said "Look here, I never heard nobody talk dat way,
I don't know 'xactly what you mean
But Mister Jenkins I must say"

Dem loving words sound mighty good to me
Dey makes me jest as happy as can be
Way down in the bottom of ma heart,
Dey makes dat loving feelin' start,
Dem loving words sound mighty good to me

The dusky wooer soon perceived,
That he was "making good,"
And so he thought he'd smear it on
As thickly as he could
He told her that her eyes were stars,
And that her teeth were pearls,
That she was like an angel child,
Compared to other girls;
She moved up closer to his side,
His arm slipped round her waist,
And then from off her pouting lips,
He slyly took a taste,
He handed out a few more lines of honey talk and then,
She threw both arms around his neck, and then she said to him
    again

Dis ain't no Time for an Argument (1906)

Words: James Weldon Johnson
Music: Rosamond Johnson

One gloomy night down thro' the woods
Old Moses Jenkins went;
He had a dog and so it seemed
He was on 'possum bent
They sneaked along and soon the dog
Barked up a 'simmon tree;
Old Moses said 'Dat sho-ly means some possum meat for me"
He quickly climbed the tree, but just imagine his surprise,
When not a possum, but a bear loomed up before his eyes
The bear he growled, and seemed to say,
"Now Moses 'twixt you and me
We'll argue out the question as to which one owns the tree."
But Moses cried in haste, "Lord, I ain't go a minute to waste."

"Dis ain't no time for an argument
Dat's plain as plain can be
Jes gimme a chance for to hit de ground,
And you can have de tree;
'Cause bear and possum meat, you see
Never did taste alike to me
Dis ain't no time for an argument
Mister Bear farewell to thee

Another night Mose had a dream
About a pot of gold;
To dig at twelve o'clock at night
By a big tree he was told.
He took a spade and went to work,
He dug thro' clay and rocks,
A smile spread over Moses, when he struck a big long box
But when he took the cover off his blood got freezing cold
For in that box he saw some things that did not look like gold
Just then a ghostly form appeared,
And said in chilling tones,
"Now Moses, we will argue, and I'll prove these are my bones."
Mose said as he begun,
For to get himself together to run

"Dis ain't no time for an argument
Dat's plain as plain can be
You say dese bones belong to you,
Wid dat I will agree;
If you wanter argue wid me 'bout dese bones,
We'll use long distance telephones,
Dis ain't no time for an argument,
Mister Ghost farewell to thee"

Don't Butt In (1901)

Words: Bob Cole and James Weldon Johnson
Music: Rosamond Johnson

Ole Moses Green gwine to vent his spleen
On a certain individual of color
Now he declares
And he daily swears
Dat he's gwine to prove dat he's a man of valor
Dere ain't no doubt dat it came about
On account of Miss Malinda his intended
She went to walk,
And she stopped to talk
With another beau and Mose he got offended;
There's trouble now
There's gwine to be a row
Mose never thought dat it was out of place
To join de conversation
When he dipped in
The trouble did begin,
For the other darkey to him said:

There's a little lesson dat you must learn,
"Don't Butt In"
When you see me busy you must wait your turn
An "Don't Butt In"
When you see me talkin' don't hang around,
If I need you I know where you can be found;
Hate it mighty bad for you to call you down,
But "Don't Butt In"

Moses swore that he'd have the gore
Of the fellow who had turned him down so boldly
He made a bluff
And got treated rough
And besides his lady love dismissed him coldly
Mose heard it said dat she was to wed
So he thought he'd go around and stop the marriage
And so dat night,
He dressed out of sight
And den drove up to de wedding in a carriage;
The preacher said
This party now will wed
Moses arose an' den without a cause began to state objections;
He raised a shout,
The people threw him out,
An' de dusky bridegroom loudly sang:

There's a little lesson dat you must learn,
"Don't Butt In"
When you see me busy you must wait your turn
An "Don't Butt In"
When you see me talkin' don't hang around,
If I need you I know where you can be found;
Hate it mighty bad for you to call you down,
But "Don't Butt In"

Don't Wake Him Up Let Him Dream (1904)

Words: James Weldon Johnson
Music: Bob Cole

Baby's asleep in his cradle
Covered with down and with lace
Look at the dear little darling
See the sweet smile on his face!
Baby is wand'ring in dreamland
Wonderful visions he sees
Princess and fairies and bright golden stairies
And mama says 'Don't wake him please!"

Don't wake up! Let him dream, dream
Dream on the whole day long!
Lovely his visions may seem, seem
To wake him would be wrong
Dreaming perhaps of some angelic group
I don't think he's dreaming of measles and croup
So don't wake him up! Let him dream, dream,
Dream, dream, dream!

Baby is out of the cradle
Now he's a boy almost 'steen"
See him way up in the tree top
Eating the apples so green
Little boy tires of his playing
Soon he lies down and he sleeps
Then gently stealing a strange funny feeling
All though his anatomy creeps

Don't wake him up! Let him dream, dream
Dream on the whole day long!
Lovely his visions may seem, seem
To wake him would be wrong
He's playing circus in his little cot
He's trying to tie himself up in a knot
So don't wake him up! Let him dream, dream
Dream, dream, dream

Sweet wedding bells they are ringing
See the young man and the maid
Marchin' away to the altar
So many plans they have laid
For they have read in the dreambook
Just how the flat can be run
Joys more extensive and life less expensive
And that two can live cheaper than one

Don't wake them up! Let them dream, dream,
Dream on the whole day long!
Lovely their visions may seem, seem
To wake him would be wrong
Dreaming six fifty a week will keep two
But won't they wake up when the flat rent is due
So don't wake him up! Let him dream, dream
Dream, dream, dream

Down in Mulberry Bend (1904)

Words: James Weldon Johnson
Music: Rosamond Johnson

There is a place on the East side
Where to watch the kids play is a treat
Children are there without number,
And it seems that they own the whole street
Though they are Poverty's children
Yet the moments are golden they spend;
And I'd like to be just a kid gay and free,
With them down in Mulberry Bend

Down in Mulberry Bend,
Down in Mulberry Bend
Life would be a picnic for me,
If one of the kids I could be,
Down in Mulberry Bend,
Where the children have fun without end
If I had my way just a kid I would stay
Down in Mulberry Bend

Kids of the Bend never worry
About what kind of playmates to choose,
Whether their clothes are in patches,
About whether or not they wear shoes
They never heard of the op'ra,
But the hand organ man is their friend
And when he comes 'round then the sidewalks resound
With laughter in Mulberry Bend

NOTE: On Sheet Music:

"Klaw and Erlanger's Production of the Greatest of all London
Drury Lane Spectacles: "Humpty Dumpty" by Cole and Johnson
Bros.
"Sambo and Dinah" sung by Mr. John McVeigh and Miss
Lillian Coleman

Other songs listed on sheet music:
"Mexico" Sung by Miss Maude Lillian Berri
"On Lalawana's Shore" sung by Miss Maude Lillian Barrl
"Down in Mulberry Bend" sung by Miss Nellie Daly
"Pussy and the Bow-Wow" sung by Mr. John McVeigh and
Miss Nellie Daly
"Welcome" sung by Mr. Frank Moulan
"Man! Man! Man!" Sung by Mr. Frank Moulan

Jos. W. Stern & Co.
34 East 21st St. NY NY
Mark Stern Building

Book by J.J.McNally
Staged by Herbert Gresham and Ned Wayburn

Written on a second copy of sheet music:
"Mulberry Bend" as sung in Sydney Rosenfeld's Musical
Comedy *The Supper Club* as produced by The Messrs Sire at
their Winter Garden, New York Theater.

Song listed on sheet music cover:
"The Maiden With the Dreamy Eyes"
"When the Band Plays Ragtime"
"When de Jack O'Lantern Starts to Walk About"
"Believe What Hubby Tells You"
"Don't Butt In" (Seabrooke's version)

"The Old Flag Never Touched the Ground"
Echoes of the Day (Daylight is Fading) (1903)

Words: James Weldon Johnson
Music: Rosamond Johnson

Daylight is fading, down goes the sun
Darkies all saying, "Our work is done!"
Old moon is peeping over de hill
All 'round de old plantation is still
'Ceptin de old screechy-owl dat hoots now and den
And de old hog a grunting Uhgh! Uhgh! Uhh! down in de pen
Work is all over, don't do no more!
Jes sit 'round and talk, near de old cabin door
Work is all over, don't do no more!
Jes sit 'round and talk, near de old cabin door

NOTE: Poem before music:

The day dies, and the cooling shades of night
Fall, as the humble slaves return from toil;
Day brings its tasks, but when it takes its flight
Rest comes, to bless these children of soil
J. W. Johnson

Elysium (1914)

Words: James Weldon Johnson
Music: Harry T. Burleigh

Your lips to mine
My heart's desire
Let my soul thrill to their passionate fire
The world melts away
In the glow of your kiss
And leaves just you and me
This perfect hour of bliss
Your lips again
Press them to mine
One more full draught of their nectarous wine
In the fold of your arms
Lull me softly until
There comes the wondrous calm of love so deep and still

Ev'ry Woman's Eyes (1912)

Words: James Weldon Johnson
Music: J. Rosamond Johnson

Though a girl is not a raving beauty
She has a way the game of love to play
For she knows that it becomes her duty
If she is wise to use her eyes
Though her nose may not be Grecian,
Nor her teeth of pearl
Though no lips of crimson ruby she can prize
Yet she has a secret that belongs to ev'ry girl
And she can use it if she tries

In ev'ry woman's eyes
The magic secret lies
No matter what their hue,
They may be black or brown or blue
And ev'ry movement shows
That ev'ry woman knows
That there's a hypnotizing charm
That lies in ev'ry woman's eyes

Just suppose a fellow's rather bashful
Look at him so
'Twill set is heart a-glow
But suppose that he is rather mashful!
Then slightly frown
And droop them down
There are times it's well to use a little naughty wink
And at other times to roll them to the skies
Or a saintly glance will often make a fellow think
That he has found his Paradise

There's a look to picture each emotion
The merry glances
The sad and dreamy trance
From flirtation up to true devotion
Can be expressed
Or half confessed
It's a woman's secret art to teach them what to say
When to shyly droop them down or make them dance
And when she decides to use them in the proper way
Where is the man who has a chance?

Everybody Wants to See the Baby (1903)

Words: James Weldon Johnson
Music: Bob Cole

Do you all know Tommy Tompkins?
Well he married just about a year ago (How lovely)
Now he has a little baby (My!)
So Tommy's quite a happy man you know (Happy Tommy)
Tommy's quite a happy man you know
Now the baby looks the same as any baby in a bed
His face just like a beet and not a hair upon his head,
Not a tooth within his mouth but always crying to be fed
Yet everybody flocks to see the baby
(Yes, everybody flocks to see the baby)

Everybody wants to see the baby,
Everybody calls him "Little dear"
When they leave they say "Great Scott!
What a homely kid they've got"
Yet everybody wants to see the baby

May be mamma takes the baby (Where?)
To an afternoon recital where they sing! (How thoughtful!)
Everybody loves the cherub (Yes)
And calls it "such a darling little thing"
(Such a darling!)
And calls it "Such a little darling thing"
But the prima donna's solo puts the cherub in a fret
And baby thinks 't would be improved if sung as a duet,
And while all are trying to listen, starts to yelling,
 then you bet
That everybody wants to choke the baby
(That everybody wants to choke the baby)

Everybody wants to choke the baby
Everybody calls him "little brat"
When the baby starts to yell
They all wish him in-oh well
Everybody wants to choke the baby

Now does papa love the baby? (Sure!)
Then why doesn't papa always show his love
(What a question!)
For it often seems that papa (Well?)
Wishes that he never saw the little dove (Never saw him)
Wishes that he never saw the little dove
For if he's been roaming with the boys and stumbles in at four,
And just as he gets into bed, the baby starts to roar,
And then mama says, "You take him John, and walk him 'round
    the floor,"
Then papa doesn't want to hold the baby
(Then papa doesn't want to hold the baby)

Papa never wants to hold the baby
Papa never wants to walk the floor
When the baby's got the croup
Papa wants to "fly the coop"
Oh Papa never wants to hold the baby

Now the baby may be peevish (Yes!)
And her temper it may go from bad to worse (Quite likely)
Up until the time of school days (Well!)
It may be very hard to keep a nurse (May be very)
It may be very hard to keep a nurse.
But if baby grows good looking, when her infant days are o'er
When she has reached the charming age of sweet sixteen or
      more,
It is very safe to bet that she'll have nurses by the score
For every fellow wants to hold the baby
For every fellow wants to hold the baby

Every fellow wants to hold the baby,
Every fellow calls her 'baby mine,"
If the baby is a "she,"
He wants to hold the baby on his knee
Yes, every fellow wants to hold the baby

If the baby sits too often (Well?)
In the parlor on a handsome fellow's knee (What happens?)
With the gas light burning dimly (Oh!)
What will happen is not hard to see (What will happen?)
What will happen is not hard to see
Oh, it means he'll ask for papa for a moment's interview
A wedding and a honeymoon, and soon as that is through,
A cozy little nest in which they live a year or two
And the baby holds another baby
And then the baby holds another baby

Then the baby holds another baby
Holds a little baby all her own
But double trouble then begins
If the baby should be twins
For it takes a couple then to hold the baby.

Excuse Me Mister Moon (1912)

Words: James Weldon Johnson
Music: J. Rosamond Johnson

Two lovers were wooing and turtle dove cooing,
The moon was just peeping o'er the hill;
The fellow felt "yummy," the girl rather chummy,
She cuddled up closer to him still,
He hugged her and kissed her, but not like a sister,
The moon looked embarrassed and ashamed;
His glance it was freezing, but the fellow kept squeezing,
And very politely he exclaimed,

Oh won't you please excuse me,
Won't you please excuse me Mister Moon!
I've got the girl, the time the place,
And I want a chance to spoon.
Just hide our face behind a cloud or two,
Then you won't be shocked at anything we do
Oh! Won't you, won't you please
Excuse me, Mister Moon

The stars were a winking, the moon he was blinking,
A soft cooling breeze began to blow,
The girl said, "Oh Willie, I feel rather chilly,
Just put both your arms around me so,"
He did to the letter, she said "I feel better,"
And close to his face she laid her head,
The moon he turned yellow,
So then once more the fellow,
Looked up with a smile to him and said

Fishing

Words: James Weldon Johnson
Music: Rosamond Johnson

No doubt you've seen a fisherman
With rod and line and hook
Sit down for hours and curse his luck,
Beside some shady brook;
He caught no fish, altho' he sat from early morn til late
And just because he didn't use the proper kind of bait

Fishing, fishing is one of the gent-lest arts,
Whether you fish for fishes,
Or whether you fish for hearts;
Fishing, fishing is not in the hands of fate
But all your success, you will find more or less,
Depends on the kind of bait.

To gentle fisher maidens too,
It may be well to state,
That diff'rent kinds of fish require,
A diff'rent kind of bait;
With backward fish, be rather pert,
With bold fish, be demure,
Select the bait to suit the fish,
The catch will then be sure.

Just what will land a fish, that's shy,
Is often hard to say,
Sometime an intellectual air,
Sometimes a childish way;
Sometimes a trick of smiling eyes,
Sometimes a saintly face,

Sometimes the glimpse of just a bit of stocking or of lace.
Some fisher maids in summer time
Go down beside the sea,
And some for mountain streams depart,
To seek the fishery
Some cast for minnows, some for whales,
And fish of great renown;
The wise girl stays at home to catch
The lobster here in town

Four fisher girls went out to fish
With rod and line and reel,
The young girl played for goldfish,
And the widow fished for eel;
The bright clever girl for crawfish tried,
With patience, skill and vim,
The old maid fish'd for anything
That had the nerve to swim

Floating Down the Nile (1906)

Words: James Weldon Johnson
Music: J. Rosamond Johnson

Sometimes I close bofe of ma eyes,
An' in ma dreams
Go to a land love where we bofe could be happy side by side
And there on a beautiful river so it seems,
In a canoe dear
We go floating together on the tide
Seems like it's a land where we lived ages ago
And dat I loved you
Even den as I love you now today
Seems like ev'ry thing dat I dream used to be so
Once in dat lan' dear on dat beautiful river far away

And then on dat river which flows down to de sea,
We float together and your dear little han' in mine I hold
And you wid yo' face near ma own listen to me
As I repeat dear that sweet story which never has grown old
Never do I go to this fair country alone,
You are beside me and we wander together han' in hand
Ah! Love it is then dat I feel you are my own,
When you and I dear are away in this fairy wonderland

Moonlight always takes me, again back to de scenes
Where we were happy and contented together you and I
Starlight never glistens above but dat it means
Lookin' again love in the beautiful love light of your eye;
Sunshine makes me think of the warmth of your true love,
It ever guides me safely on though the storm may wreck an' roar,
And love when the evening of life falls from above,
May we go drifting han' in han' as we did in days of yore.

Gimme De Leavin's (1904)

Words: James Weldon Johnson
Music: Bob Cole

I've never had exactly what I'd like to have in life
Although I think I've had my share of troubles and of strife
I've never had a chance to see the things I'd like to see
Somehow the good things all run out before they get to me
The stronger I reach for a thing, the father it goes off
The hardest jobs all look for me while others git the sof'
So in de future if a good thing comes along my way
And den, as usual, pass me by, I'm simply gwine to say

Gimme de leavin's when you get through
Jes gimme de leavin's and dat will do
Man wants but a little bit here below
Smaller my little bit seems to grow
I got so now I don't look for no mo'
Dan de leavins'
Gimme de leavins'

One night I put my bes' clothes on and went to see my gal
I took a watermelon as a present for my Sal
I thought about de pleasant time dere was for me in sto'
A eating watermelon and a kissin' mo an'mo'
When I got dere I thought I'd give my gal a big surprise
So I slipped right in thoo de do- an' dere be fo' my eyes
I se'ed her jes a hugging and a kissing my friend Ned
I dropped my melon on de flo' and mournfully I said

I've had a hard time traveling long the rocky road of life
I've run against so many snags and stumbling blocks of strife
Old Hard Luck followed at my heels, until one day behold!
I found a pocket book chock full of bright and shiny gold
I put the gold beneath my head and went to sleep tonight
Such happy dreams! When all at once I woke up with a fright
A burglar had my bag of gold, my poor heart filled with pain
I couldn't move, he had me tied, I begged him all in vain

The Glory of the Day Was in Her Face (1925)

Words: James Weldon Johnson
Music: Harry T. Burleigh

The glory of the day was in her face
The beauty of the night was in her eyes
And over all her lovliness
And over all her loveliness
The grace of morning blushing, blushing in the early skies

And in her voice the calling of the dove
Like music of a sweet melodious part
And in her smile the breaking light of love
And all the gentle virtues in her heart
And now the glorious day, the beauteous night
The birds that signal to their mates at dawn
To my dull ears to my tear-blind sight
Are one with all the dead
Since she has gone

Hello Ma Lulu (1905)

Words: James Weldon Johnson
Music: Rosamond Johnson

I don't wait for no moon to shine
No stars for to shed der light
But goes ev'ry evenin' for to see ma gal
No matter how dark de night
I don't take no banjo along
Don't try no songs to squeak,
I talks to her just good and plain
And dese am de words I speak:

Hello ma Lula! Ma Lulu
Lu I call 'round dis evenin' to see how you do;
I'm feeling lonely, if you is too
I'll be yo' honey boy,
You'll be ma Lu!"

"Singing Sammy" and "Banjo Joe"
Have tried for to win my Lu,
And both of 'em knows dat in harmony
Der's nothin' dat I can do
Lulu smiles while both of 'em tries
To rival de mocking birds
But she forgets dat harmony
As soon as she heard dese words

I don't 'spect for to waste no time
To learn how to play and sing,
I've made up my mind dat for to win a gal
Sweet talk is de proper things
Lulu's promised she will be mine
Dat's 'xactly what she's done
I'se win'd her for my June-time bride
And dese am de words dat won:

Her Eyes Twin Pools (1915)

Words: James Weldon Johnson
Music: Harry T. Burleigh

Her eyes, twin pools of mystic light
Soft star-sheen melting into night
O'er which, to sound their glam'rous haze,
A man might bend, and vainly gaze
Her eyes, twin pools so dark and deep
In which life's ancient myst'ries sleep;
Wherein to seek the quested goal,
A man might plunge, and lose his soul,
 Lose his soul
A man might plunge and lose his soul

I Ain't Gwine Ter Work No More (1900)

Words: Bob Cole and James Weldon Johnson
Music: Rosamond Johnson

Hard time, money is scarce as scarce can be
No job, no chance; its all de same to me
I don't worry about de way things run,
Takes life easy; I finds its heap mo' fun
Once I had a dead swell job a working on Broadway
A little bit of work each day,
For which I used to draw big pay
I lost dat job, and got dead broke,
I don't know who's to blame
I'm loafing now, but somehow or 'nother
I'm a living just the same

So I ain't gwine ter work no mo'
Labor is tiresome sho'
The best occupation is recreation;
Life's mighty short, you know
No use to pinch and save
You can't take it to the grave
Peter won't know if you rich or po'
So I ain't gwin ter work no mo'

Dey say all things will come to dem dat wait
An' I'm willing to get mine at dat rate
Rich folks worry about de wealth dey got
Po' folks dey grieve about der sorry lot
I don't see de use of work,
'cause if you rich or po'
You keep a working hard for mo'
You never git enough, you know;
So what's de use of working hard
You can't be satisfied,
You jes well take things jes like you find em
Dis is why I done de side

Dat I ain't gwine ter work no mo'
Labor is tiresome sho'
The best occupation is recreation;
Life's mighty short, you know
No use to pinch and save
You can't take it to the grave
Peter won't know if you rich or po'
So I ain't gwinter work no mo'

I Don't Want to Be No Actor Man No Mo' (1901)

Words: James Weldon Johnson and Rosamond Johnson
Music: Bob Cole

Bill Jones was doing well,
As porter in a big hotel
'Till the owner of a show stopped there one day,
He said to Bill, "I see you have ability,
And talent and you ought to make it pay"
Bill took this tip and all the tips
That he for years had saved,
And organized a minstrel show
To be an actor man he craved,
He said, "I'll be the Black Shakespeare,
I'll play Macbeth or 'bust,'"
They stranded ninety miles from home
Then Bill said in disgust,

I don't want to be no actor man, no mo'
I'm through troopin' wid de Darktown minstrel sho'
I got enough a lookin' for a great big name
No mo' searchin' for yo empty fame,
I don't want to be no actor man no mo'

Besides a railroad track
He sadly watched the trains go back,
To the place where he once ate three meals a day
A tear bedimmed Bill's eye, he heaved a mournful sigh,
As the dusky actors dunned him for their pay

For three long days Bill tried his best to get identified,
'Till at last he met a man he knew before
He got the cash alright, his troup screamed with delight,
For they saw themselves back home to leave no more
So gladly with their grips in hand, they started for the train,
Bill jumped aboard all by himself of course that made it plain,
That he had fare for only one, and as he waved back to the gang,
The actors wiped their weeping eyes, and in a chorus sang:

I've Got Troubles of My Own (1900)

Words: Bob Cole and James Weldon Johnson
Music: Rosamond Johnson

Since I been a deacon in de Bab-tist church
I'm bothered 'most to death;
De darkies come around me wid der hard luck tales
And talks me out o' breath
Keeps myself se-clud-ed, but it ain't no use,
Dey's bound to find me, sho'!
F'om early mawn-in to late at eb-nin;
Some hard luck Eth-i-o-pian's at my do'
Jes' dis mawnin as day was dawnin'
Here comes old Hezekiah Brown
Says his quaint-en-ces and re-la-tion-ces had all throwed him
    down;
Out o' money done lost his job,
He has two months house rent for to pay;
He requested dat I assist him, but to Mister Brown I had to say

I've got troubles of my own!
G'way, leave me alone!
My friend, can't you see dat I'm jess busy as I can be?
His tale might a been true
His rent might a been due,
But my rent was due too
I've got troubles of my own

Seems to me dat ev'ry darkey in dis town
Must bring his griefs to me
As long as dey live easy and der paths run smooth
Dey shuns my 'ci-e-ty
Bein' a convenience for dese
Dead broke coons will put me on de shelf
I'm gwin' ter cul-ti-vate other 'so-ci-ates,
So I can borrow now and then, my-self
Jes' dis evenin' as I was leavin' a crowd of hungry looking Japs
Who should 'proach me but brother Eph-ra-ham just through
    shootin' craps
Lost his wages and scared to go home because he knew his wife
    would fuss
He requested dat I assist him, but I spoke to Eph-ra-ham a thus:

I've got troubles of my own!
Go 'way, leave me a-lone
My friend can't you see
Dat I'm jess busy as I can be?
His tale might a been true
But what could I a do?
I'm scared to go home too
I've got troubles of my own

Dis here takin' me for a free-lan-tho-fist is cert'-ny got to stop
It seems to me de darkies got it in der heads
Dat I'm a free pond-shop
Sho-ly will inform 'em, and inform 'em quick
Dat friendship bank's done bust!
I'm gwin ter no-ti-fy dese glad-hand coons
Dat I don't in-tend to run no trouble trust!

While a-nappin' I heard a rappin' last night upon my window pane
Raised de window, dere was Abe Washington standin' in de rain
Wife deserted him, car'd off ev'-ry-thing
Swore she never would come back
He requested dat I persuade her,
So to Abe I had to 'cite dis fack:

I've got troubles of my own!
Go 'way, leave me a-lone!
My friend can't you see dat I'm jess busy as I can be?
His tale might a been true
And he might a felt a blue
But I'm a grass widower too, I've got troubles of my own!

If the Sands of the Seas Were Pearls (1904)

Words: James Weldon Johnson
Music: Will Marion

Since I have looked into your eyes
And seen the love light in them shine,
I know I've found my paradise,
You love me and the world is mine
The treasure of your love I'll hold
Till all the stars burn dim above;
Not for a world of wealth untold
Would I exchange your priceless love

If the sands of all the seas were peerless pearls,
If the rocks of all the hills were purest gold
If they were mine alone
And I could call my own
The treasures that the earth and ocean hold,
If the keeping of these countless riches cost
That your love to me should be forever lost
My soul's desire, I'd count these boundless riches all too few
I'd give them all and hold just you

Though riches of the world be won
Without love's jewel they are dross,
And when the weary years are done
We find that all is bitter loss
Oh, sweetheart, you have taught me this
You've taught me what it is to live;
Your love alone holds perfect bliss,
Alone holds all that life can give.

If the sands of all the seas were peerless pearls
If the rocks of all the hills were purest gold
If they were mine alone
And I could call my own
The treasures that the earth and ocean hold
If the keeping of these countless riches cost
That your love to me should be forever lost
My soul's desire, I'd count these boundless riches all too few
I'd give them all and hold just you

If You'll Be My Eve (I'll Build An Eden For You) (1912)

Words: James Weldon Johnson
Music: J. Rosamond Johnson

Said a blushing youth to a maid one day,
There is something dear, I wish to say to you,
   Just you
And the maid though undesigning
Like her sex was quite divining
So she drooped her eyes and bowed her modest head
While the ardent lover took her hand and said

If you'll be my Eve
I'll build an Eden for you
A Garden of Eden all for you
With roses red to say how much I love you
And violets to say that I'll be true
Sweet heart, then come with me and be just my own
I'll give all my love to you alone
If you will be my Eve I'll build an Eden for you
A Garden of Eden all for you

Then the maiden lifted her drooping head
And her eyes grew moist, her cheeks blush'd red like a rose
   A rose
But her heart had long been guessing
What the youth was then confessing
For the same sweet song has been the song of man
From the first young lover since the world began

The Katy-did, the Cricket and the Frog (1903)

Words: James Weldon Johnson
Music: Bob Cole

An old bull frog who was rather gay,
Met a pretty Katy-did,
She caught his fancy right away,
For her heart he made a bid
Said he to her, "although my back is green,
Yet my green backs are not few
If you'll agree to abide with me,
There'll be no thing too good for you, you, you
There'll be nothing too good for you."

And so that night in the pale moonlight,
The Katy-did
She listen'd to the frog
While he tried to woo, and to bill and coo,
As the two sat together on a log, log, log,
The pretty little Katy and the frog

One day the frog met a cricket friend,
'Twas a chance he couldn't miss
To give his friend his private views
On connubial joy and bliss
Said he to him, 'Now would you like to know why
Such happiness fills my eye?
Just come with me to my mossy bank
And I'll show you the reason why, why, why
And I'll show you the reason why."

And so that night in the pale moonlight
The Katy-did, the cricket and the frog,
Had a lively chat about this and that,
As the three sat together on the log, log, log
The Katy-did, the cricket and the frog

The cricket he was a dandy thing,
And he charm'd the Katy-did;
His dress was fine, he talked and sang,
While the moon in silence hid
The bull frog dozed, the cricket said,
"I think all the views he expressed are true."
Then whisper'd something in Katy's ear,
And together away they flew, flew, flew
And together away they flew

And so that night in the pale moonlight,
A sad and gloomy picture was the frog,
He bemoan'd his fate at a lively rate
As he sat alone upon the log, log, log,
A poor forsaken but a wiser frog

Lay Away Your Troubles (1903)

Words: James Weldon Johnson
Music: Bob Cole

When old Mister Sun gets tired a-hangin' round and round de sky;
When der ain't no thunder and lightnin' a bangin'
And de crops am all laid by;
When your bones ain't achin' wid de rhe-ma-tics,
Den you ride de mule to town
Get a great big jug of de apple juice
And when you drink her down

Jes lay away your troubles and dry up all your tears,
'Cause den your pleasure doubles,
And you're sure to lose your keers,
You lay away your sorrow high up upon de shelf
And never mind to tomorrow
'Twill take care of it self

When old Mister Age he comes a-stealin'
Through your back and knees,
When your bones and joints lose der limber-like feelin'
And am stiff-nin' by degrees
Now der's but one way to feel a-young and spry
When you hear dem banjos soun'
Get a great big swig of de apple juice,
And when you drink her down

Jes lay away your troubles, and dry up all your tears,
'Cause den your pleasure doubles,
And you're sure to lose your keers,
You lay away your sorrow high up upon de shelf
And never mind tomorrow
'Twill take care of itself

NOTE: At top of the sheet music:

De cotton it has done been picked, de 'taters dey's been dug
Der's grub enough for ev'ry pickaninny;
Come gadder 'round and first we'll drink de essence of de jug
And den we'll dance de "Essence of Virginny."
J.W. Johnson

Also on sheet music:
"The First of the Cole and Johnson Negro Songs" "The four songs of which this is the first, are supposed to illustrate the growth of the forms of negro music from the old days of minstrelsy to the present day. The first song represents a typical minstrel song of the olden days."

Bottom of sheet music: "In the next (June) Journal, Messrs. Cole and Johnson will present a song of an entirely different character, called "Darkies' Delights," introducing the famous refrain of "Carve dat Possum," illustrating a song typical of the old cabin plantation days. –The Editors.

James Weldon Johnson

Lift Every Voice and Sing

Words: James Weldon Johnson
Music: J. Rosamond Johnson

Lift every voice and sing,
Till earth and heaven ring,
Ring with the harmonies of liberty;
Let our rejoicing rise
High as the listening skies,
Let it resound loud as the rolling sea.
Sing a song full of the faith
That the dark past has taught us,
Sing a song full of the hope
That the present has brought us;
Facing the rising sun of our new day begun,
Let us march on till victory is won.

Stony the road we trod,
Bitter the chastening rod,
Felt in the days when hope unborn had died;
Yet with a steady beat,
Have not our weary feet come to the place
For which our fathers died?

We have come over a way
That with tears have been watered,
We have come, treading our path
Through the blood of the slaughtered,
Out from the gloomy past,
Till now we stand at last
Where the white gleam of our bright star is cast.

God of our weary years,
God of our silent tears,

- 112 -

Thou who hast brought us thus far on the way;
Thou who hast by thy might led us into the light,
Keep us forever in the path, we pray.

Lest our feet stray from the places,
Our God, where we met thee;
Lest our hearts drunk with the wine of the world
We forget thee,
Shadowed beneath thy hand, may we forever stand
True to our God, true to our naïve land.

A school program was planned in Jacksonville to celebrate President Abraham Lincoln's birthday on February 12, 1900. James Weldon Johnson was scheduled to give an address and decided to also write a song for the occasion. With his brother, Rosamond, composing the melody, James Johnson wrote the lyrics to "Lift Every Voice." The song quickly caught on with schools, churches and then NAACP meetings until it became known as the "Negro National Anthem." The song continues to be performed by African-American choirs and soloists at special events.

Louisiana Lize (1899)

Words and Music: James Weldon Johnson and Rosamond Johnson
Composed: Bob Cole

All de time I'm working
I'm a-thinking 'bout my darling down de ribber cross de way
Thinking 'bout my sugar plum and wonders if she loves me
All de nighttime, all de day
Sometime my heart gits in a flurry
Sometime my head begins to worry
Thinking 'bout my Louisiana Lize

Dat gal wid de purty shiny eyes, my Lize
Dem eyes!
Dey cause my blood to rise

I wonder if she really loves me
I'd like to know
I wonder if she really knows dat I love her so
She's jes as sweet as 'lasses candy
She's jes my size
I wonder, I ponder
All de time about my lubly Lize
My Lize, dem eyes
My Louisiana Lize

Everything around de ole plantation
Seems to tell me dat my darling lubs me true
All de birds a-singing, an' de bumble bees a-hummin'
Don't you worry she lubs you
Night time I starts my boat to floatin'
Nighttime dats when I goes a cotin'
Goes to cote my Louisiana Lize
Dat gal wid de purty shiny eyes, my Lize
Dem eyes!
Dey cause my blood to rise

Before James and Rosamond Johnson left New York to return to Jacksonville after their first songwriting trip in the summer of 1899, they wrote "Louisiana Lize" with Bob Cole. On the sheet music with Lottie Gibson on the cover, the song is credited as "composed by Bob Cole." Words and Music edited by J.W. and Rosamond Johnson but on the sheet music with May Irwin on the cover it states "composed by Bob Cole. Words and Music by J.W. and Rosamond Johnson." James Weldon Johnson noted that May Irwin purchased the singing rights to the song for $50.

Lovely Daughter of Allah (An Arabian Episode) (1912)

Words: James Weldon Johnson
Music: J. Rosamond Johnson

Over the desert sand
In a palace grand
Lived a Sultan's daughter
She was the Sultan's pride
And the promised bride
Of a Caliph old
But by a secret way
Came a youth one day
To the sultan's garden
And 'neath her window there
To the Princess fair,
Love's story told

Lovely daughter of Allah!
By the stars above you,
I swear I love you
Won't you love me?
Come to my arms, dear
Let me enfold you
My love is deeper than the deep blue sea
Lovely daughter of Allah

Bright was the Caliph's gold
But his heart was cold
As his yellow treasure
But like a flame of fire
Was the love desire
Of the youth so bold
So when the Sultan came
His be-lov'd to claim
She had gone forever
Gone from the palace grand
O'er the burning sand
T'is the story old

Ma Mississippi Belle (1902)

Words and Music: Cole and Johnson Bros.

Down de Mississippi, where de steamboats run
Der's a landin' dat I know so well
Where de southern breeze slumbers in de trees
Live a little gal I call ma belle
Standin' on de landin' is ma sugar plum
When de steamboat puts in for de sho'
Sweet as sweet can be
Waitin' dere for me
When she hears dat whistle blow
Boo-oo-oo-oo
Boo-o--oo-oo
Boo-oo-oo-oo-oo-oo

Ma Mississippi belle, ma belle
Ma darling, won't you tell
Oh, tell me if your love ma turtle dove
Is only goin' to linger for a spell?
Ma Mississippi belle, ma belle
I loves you mighty well, so well
Yes, and to you I will be true
Ma Mississippi belle, ma belle

When we makes de landin' an' I gits a show
Close I goes a cote-in' of my belle
Eyes as big an bright as de stars at night
How I love dat gal no tongue can tell
If dis pretty little gal will marry me
I won't go back on dat boat no mo'
Cause it breaks her heart dat we have to part
When we hear dat whistle blow

Ma Mississippi belle, ma belle
Ma darling, won't you tell
Oh, tell me if your love ma turtle dove
Is only goin' to linger for a spell?
Ma Mississippi belle, ma belle
I loves you mighty well, so well
Yes, and to you I will be true
Ma Mississippi belle, ma belle

Magdaline, My Southern Queen

Words and Music: Bob Cole and Johnson Bros.

All the stars are twinkling in the skies above
My Magdaline, my Magdaline,
And my heart is longing now to tell its love for you,
My Queen, My Southern Queen.
While the moon is shining with its silv'ry light
And the orange blossoms scent perfumes the night
And the gentle breeze murmurs to the trees,
'Tis the time, my love, our vows to plight

Oh, come, Oh, do!
I plead to you!
For I'm wanting and I'm watching, love, for you

Won't you come with me, my Magdalene?
The night serene invites my queen
Come, and promise you'll be mine,
And I'll worship at your shrine!
Won't you come and be my Southern Queen!

All the birds are singing songs of love
You, you, My Magdaline, my Magdaline,
Ev'ry thing in nature tries your heart to woo for me,
My Queen, My southern Queen,
Come, I'm waiting darling, with my little boat
Down the stream of life together love, we'll float,
'Tis my fondest dream!
Will you reign supreme?
All my life, to you I will devote
Oh, come! Oh, do! I plead to you!
For I'm wanting and I'm watching, love, for you

The Maid of Timbuctoo (1903)

Words: James Weldon Johnson
Music: Bob Cole.

In Africa's sunny land,
Beyond the desert's sand,
There lived a maid, I've heard it said,
In a place called Timbuctoo
Bold chieftains by the score,
Would come for miles or more,
Arrayed in beads and pumpkin seeds,
This little maid to woo

The maid of Timbuctoo,
She knew just what to do,
When suitors came to woo her for her hand;
She shyly dropped her eyes
And heaved a sea of sighs,
Yet she was very wise, you understand

She was uncivilized, yet you'd have been surprised,
If you had seen that maiden green,
Taking in those Zulu guys;
She relieved them of their rings,
Their beads and other things,
In such a way, I dare to say,
They never did get wise

When e'er some chieftain fine,
Invited her to dine,
She shook her head, and shyly said:
"That to eat she did not care"
But yet she'd sit and munch
Bananas by the bunch,
And make them bring her ev'ry thing
On a Zulu bill of fare.

The Maiden With the Dreamy Eyes (1901)

Words: James Weldon Johnson
Music: Bob Cole

No doubt you've seen the maiden with the dimple in her chin
A very charming girl is she;
The maid with feet and ankles that a beauty prize would win
A very pretty sight to see
But the maiden that's most charming,
All your wariness disarming,
With seductiveness alarming
Is the maiden with the dreamy eyes

There are eyes of blue
There are brown eyes too,
There are eyes of ev'ry size, and ev'ry hue;
But I surmise, that if you are wise,
You'll be careful of the maiden with the dreamy eyes

The maiden with the dreamy eyes you cannot well resist,
There's magnetism in those eyes,
They make a fellow feel that she is longing to be kissed,
And there is where the danger lies,
Although marriage you're opposing,
When you see her eyes half closing,
You cannot resist proposing
To the maiden with the dreamy eyes

You get a-board a Broadway car and get a seat perhaps,
That's quite a lucky thing to do
While aged female passengers are hanging on the straps,
And ev'ry body stares at you,
With the crowd that still comes piling;
Comes a maid with eyes beguiling,
And you give your seat up smiling
To the maiden with the dreamy eyes

NOTE: This song was introduced in the musical *The Supper Club*, then sung by Anna Held in the musical *The Little Duchess*. Held was the wife of Florence Ziegfeld, originator and promoter of "Ziegfeld's Follies." *The Little Duchess*, a Ziegfeld production, opened at the Casino Theatre in 1901 and this became Anna Held's theme song.

Man, Man, Man (1904)

Words: James Weldon Johnson
Music: Bob Cole

For ages men have done their best to make us all believe
That all the trouble on this earth was caused by Mother Eve
But if the page of history you take the time to scan
You'll found that at the bottom of all the trouble there's a man

Man! Man! Man! Man!
He's been a bunch of trouble ever since the world began
Man! Man! Man! Man!
What's his uses tell me if you can
How does he figure in the universal plan?
Take a book and when his past performances you scan
You'll find that he is rated in the class of "also ran"
So, what's the use of man?

He's worked up all the trouble that we have, we know it's true
Besides that I should like to know what is there he can do?
I'd like to see the man who thinks
That he could stand the shocks
In trying to nurse a baby while he darned pair of socks

Now can he thread a needle, can he teach an infant class?
And could he fix his back hair up without a looking glass?
About the frail and weaker sex they very often speak
But where's the man could read thro' ten new novels in a week?

A little collar button makes him tear his hair, and rave
And what a homely thing he is when he forgets to shave!
And can he gossip scandal or can he describe a dress?
Send him to buy the baby's clothes and won't he make a mess!

Mexico (1904)

Words: Bob Cole and James Weldon Johnson
Music: Bob Cole

Over the Rio Grande,
There lies the land of sunshine
Over the Rio Grande
There lives a love of mine.

In the evening on the plaza
My little Mexican Queen
With her elderly Duenna is often seen
There I plead to her with glances
And she heaves a little sigh
And I whisper to her softly as she goes by

Mexico!—My dark-eyed Mexico!
Tho' years may come and go
I'll constant be
Oh! Mexico I dearly love you so!
And I would like to know if you love me

Mexico!—with the shade of midnight in your hair
And your smile like the sunny southern skies;
Mexico!—with the coral lips and face so fair
And the glow of the starlight in your eyes
Mexico! Can you tell me will it ever be
That your love and your heart will be my own?

Mexico!—I'll be happy if you promise me
That you'll love me alone
Oh! Mexico—my dark eyed Mexico!
Tho' years may come and go
I'll constant be
Oh! Mexico—I dearly love you so!
And I would like to know
If you love me

Morning, Noon and Night (1916)

Words: James Weldon Johnson
Music: J. Rosamond Johnson

When morning shows her first faint flush,
I think of the tender blush
That crept so gently to your cheek
When first my love I dared to speak
How in your glance a dawning ray
Gave promise of love's perfect day

When in the ardent breath of noon,
The roses with passion swoon,
There steals upon me from the air
The scent that lurked within your hair;
I touch your hand, I clasp your form,
Again your lips are close and warm

When comes the night with beauteous skies,
I think of your tar-dimmed eyes—
Their mute entreaty that I stay
Although your lips sent me away;
Then memory brings its bitter blight,
And dark, so dark becomes the night!

NOTE: On the sheet music owned by Carl Van Vechten in the Beinecke Library at Yale, Rosamond Johnson wrote, "This poem was written by Jim especially for me to set to music. It was only in manuscript at the time when Roland Hayes sang it for the first time in Carnegie Hall. The concert was for the benefit of the Music School Settlement for Colored People. Roland's rendition was superb."

My Angemima Green (1902)

Words: James Weldon Johnson
Music: Bob Cole

Listen while I tell you of my Angemime
Eyes far brighter than the stars above that shine
Graceful as a swan and with a form divine
With a style and manner superfine
Like a bright sunflower is my dusky queen
She's the neatest sweetest creature ever seen
You will understand exactly what I mean
When you see my Angemima Green

You ought to see my Angemime
She's the one that leads the line
All the other dusky damsels have to fall behind;
They just can't help when she goes by
To roll their eyes and heave a sigh
You can bet t'would do you good
To see my Angemime

It was on a balmy moonlight night in June
Angemime and I strolled out beneath the moon
And I hummed to her a little darkey croon;
Then she promised me to marry soon
It will fill my heart I know with joy and pride
When down thro' the crowded church we'll gaily glide
With my sweet and blushing charmer by my side
When I make Angemima Green my bride

My Castle On The Nile (1901)

Words: James Weldon Johnson and Bob Cole
Music: Rosamond Johnson

Dere ain't no use in try'n to rise up in de social scale
Less you kin trace yo' name back to de flood
You got to have ancestral halls an'den you mus'nt fail
To prove dere's indigo mixed in yo' blood
I done foun' out dat I come down from ole Chief Bungaboo,
My great gran-dad-y was his great gran-chile
An' so I'm gwin' ter sail away across de waters blue
To occupy my castle on de Nile

In my Castle on de river Nile
I am gwinter live in elegant style
Inlaid diamonds on de flo'
A Baboon butler at my do'
When I wed dat princess Anna Mazoo
Den my blood will change from red to blue
Entertaining royalty all the while in my castle on the Nile

I'm goin' where I kin eat de bes' an live on foreign game
Where chickens grow dey tell me six feet tall
De natives call dem ostriches no matter 'bout de name
De flavor of de meat's de same, dat's all
I'll form a royal party an' I'll hunt for elephant
"An when I fish I'll fish for crocodile
A monkey for my valet, Oh I'll live extravagant
In my ancestral castle on the Nile

NOTE: In their book, *Ragged But Right*, authors Lynn Abbott and Doug Seroff state that "Castle on the River Nile" was "a first rate example of a sophisticated turn-of-the-century ragtime coon song. While the clever lyrics are constructed around ludicrous racial allusions, they are neither crude nor unwholesome." The authors note that while presenting *The Sons of Ham* in New York during October and November, 1901, Bert Williams recorded several songs for the Victor Company, including the show's biggest hits, "The Phrenologist Coon," "My Little Zulu Babe," and "In My Castle on the Nile." The Deep River Boys recorded it in the 1940s.

My Creole Belle (1900)

Words: James Weldon Johnson
Music: Rosamond Johnson

Now if you want to see a girl
To put you in a trance,
Get one whose pedigree goes back
To flow'ry Spain or sunny France
The ragtime blood in her veins
Gives her a red hot pace,
But ev'ry move is modified by her Parisian grace
Just watch her air
So debonair
Her cakewalk prance
Is a la France

She is a belle, a Creole belle
So charming and so very swell
Just see her when she walks the street
A vision fair from head to feet
You catch a glimpse as round she flirts,
Of pretty lace and dainty skirts,
Upon your heart she puts a spell
This fascinating Creole belle

This Creole belle she sets you mad
With her bewitching smiles
Well versed is she in all the tricks
And magic of love's arts and wiles,
Your heart beats in ragtime
When you look into her eyes
And you are deep in love
With her before you realize
Just ask a kiss
She laughs like this
And flirts away to your dismay

My Heart's Desiah Is Miss Mariah (1901)

Words: Bob Cole and James Weldon Johnson
Music: Rosamond Johnson

I've got a mighty tickerlist feeling
In the region of a my heart
It's all on account of Miss Mariah,
An' I don't know how it came to start
It surely is a funny sensation,
Tho' it ain't no ache or pain;
It gives me a mighty heap of trouble,
And it's sump'n that I can't explain

My heart's desiah is Miss Mariah
She is the apple of my eye!
Sweeter than the apple when the apple's in the pie!
An' when I'm nigh her
My heart's on fi-ah!
Oh, Miss Mariah, you's my heart's desiah!

When I was introduced to Miss Mariah,
An' I looked into her eyes,
I knew that if I could ever win her,
That I'd surely have the world's first prize!
I tried my best to tell her that I loved her,
But the words refused to flow.
Just how I'm a-longing for you, honey
O, my darling, you can never know

My One and Only (1906)

Words: James Weldon Johnson
Music: Bob Cole

Love is such a funny confection
Love is such a strange infection
Love knows neither clime nor section
It's the same with young and old
Way down South so bright and sunny
Hear a darkey court his "honey"
Though his language may sound funny
It's the story often told

My one and only
I am so lonely,
Keep dreamin' 'bout you
Can't do without you
That's why I haunt you
Because I want you
To be my only
My one and only one

You may roam all over creation,
You will find in ev'ry nation
Love's the same in ev'ry station,
Though it bears a diff'rent name
Though in Scotland it is stuttered
And in Germany it's muttered
And in Spain it's lightly uttered
Still the story is the same

My Lady's Lips Am Like de Honey (1915)

Words: James Weldon Johnson
Music: Will Marion Cook

Breeze a-sighin' and a-blowin'
Southern summer night
Stars a-gleamin' and a glowin'
Moon jes' shinin' right
Strollin' like de lovers do
Long de lane and Lindy Lou
Honey on her lips to waste
'Speck I'm gwine to steal a taste

Oh, my lady's lips am like de honey
My lady's lips am like de rose
An' I am jes' like de bee
Roun' de flower where de nectah grows
Little lady's lips dey smile so temptin'
Li'l lady's teeth so white dey shine
Li'l lady's lips so tantalizin'
Oh, my lady's lips so close to mine
My lady's lips so close to mine

Bird a-whistlin' and a-swayin'
In de live oak tree
Seems to me he keeps a-sayin'
Kiss dat gal fo' me!
Look heah, Mister Mockin' bird
Gwine to take you at yo' word
If I meet a Waterloo
Gwine to blame it all on you

Honey in de rose, I s'pose
Is put dere fo' de bee
Honey on her lips, I knows
Is put dere jes fo' me
Seen a sparkle in her eye
Hyeahd her sorter heave a sigh
Felt her kinder squeeze my han'
'Nuff to make me understan'

No Use In Askin' 'Cause You Know The Reason Why (1901)

Words: James Weldon Johnson
Music: Rosamond Johnson

Mose Jenkin's wife, Amanda Jane got it into her head
To entertain her preacher wid a birthday dinner spread;
She baked a great big possum wid potatoes good and sweet
And all she lacked for to fill the bill,
Was some good chicken meat
And so she sent old Moses out to go upon the trail;
Mose found the hens but sad to say,
He got himself in jail
Next day the preacher went to him and asked why he was there;
Mose rolled his eyes at dat preacher man,
And then he did declare:

"Dere's No use in askin' 'cause you know de reason why!'
You sho' kin understand dis myst'ry if you try;
Member you had chicken meat at my house de odder day to eat?
And so dere's no use in askin' 'cause you know the reason why."

When Mose got out he told his wife what he was goin' to do,
He said dat he would surely beat dat preacher black and blue;
Mose met him on the street one day,
He said dis is my chance
So on the Reverend Jasper Brown,
He made a quick advance,
But Jasper jumped on Moses and he beat him most to death;
He blacked his eyes and bruised his nose,
Den chased him out of breath;
Somebody said "Why Hello Mose, what makes you run so fast?"
Mose did not stop, for to make reply,
But he stated as he passed:

"Dere's No use in askin' 'cause you know the reason why!
I'm only runnin' 'cause I ain't got wings to fly;
See dat preacher in de rear?
Well it's my business for to keep him dere,
And so dere's no use in askin' 'cause you know the reason why!"

Nobody's Lookin' But De Owl An' De Moon (1901)

Words: James Weldon Johnson and Bob Cole
Music: Rosamond Johnson

De ribber is a glistenin' in de moonlight,
Honey, de owl is settin' high up in de tree,
De little stars am twinklin' wida sof' light,
Honey, de night seems only jes fo' you an' me
Thro de trees de breezes am a-sighin'
Breathin' out assort o'lover's croon,
Der's nobody lookin' or a-spyin':
Nobody but de owl an' de moon

Nobody's lookin' but de owl an' de moon,
De night is balmy fo' de month is June,
Den my little Honey, Honey,
Come to meet me soon,
While nobody's lookin'
But de owl an' de moooooooooon
But de owl an' de moon

I feel so kinder lonely all de daytime, Honey,
It seems I really doan know what to do.
I jes keep sort a-longin'
Fo' de nighttime, Honey,
Cause den I knows dat I will be wid you
An' de thought jes sets my brain a-swayin'
An' my heart a-beatin' to a tune,
Come, de owl won't tell what we's a-sayin'
An' cose, you know we kin' trust de moon

O Southland (1914)

Words: James Weldon Johnson
Music: Harry T. Burleigh

O Southland, Southland
Dear land so far away
We dream of thee by night
We long for thee by day
Long years our fathers 'neath the sun
Bent under weary weight of toil
They fell'd thy forest and brought forth
All rich treasures of thy soil
And so thy sun, thy soil, thy rocks
Thy forests, streams and flow'rs
By right of birth, by right of love are ours

NOTE: "O Southland" was a poem by James Weldon Johnson that was set to music by H.T. Burleigh. Burleigh studied classical music at the New York Conservatory under the Czech composer Antonin Dvorak and introduced Dvorak to African-American folk music.

Oh Didn't He Ramble

Songwriter: Will Handy

Old Beebe had three full grown sons,
Buster, Bill and Bee
And Buster was the black sheep of the Beebe family
They tried their best to break him
Of his rough and rowdy ways,
At last they had to get a Judge to give him ninety days

Oh! Didn't he ramble, ramble?
He rambled all around, in and out of town,
Oh didn't he ramble, ramble,
He rambled till the butchers cut him down

NOTE: This song is credited to Will Handy; however, a hand-written note on the sheet music by Rosamond Johnson states, "This song was based on an old bawdy house song—we changed the melody slightly and softened the words but none of us cared to put his name on it. We invented the name of Will Handy long before W.C. Handy came on the Broadway scene. This song became the official Yale football song "He Rambled Till Old Eli Cut Him Down." The folk song this was based on was "The Darby Ram" and the version by Cole and the Johnson brothers was soon adopted by New Orleans bands and became a Dixieland standard.

Oh, You Sweet, Sweet Boy (1913)

Words: James Weldon Johnson
Music: J. Rosamond Johnson

My heart is glad, I'm never sad
I've got some angel boy
He makes the world a paradise
And he fills my heart with joy
He is so sweet
He's such a treat
When I'm beside him life for me
Is just one perfect dream
And when he fondles me I feel
So happy I could scream
I hold him near, and murmur dear

Oh! You sweet, sweet boy
You ever loving bunch of joy
Come snuggle up and cuddle down
So I can put my arms around you
Oh, you precious joy
You milk and honey boy
I want to pet you angel child
I'm just so crazy I'm running wild
About that boy
My one best joy
You sweet, sweet
Make my life complete
You sweet, sweet, sweet, sweet boy
Oh you sweet, sweet, sweet, sweet boy

Of all the joys this world can give
I love this one the best
To cuddle down into his arms
Like a birdie in its nest
To squeeze him tight
With all my might
And when he holds his lips to mine
In one long loving kiss
Right through my heart I feel the thrill
Of sweet electric bliss
I tremble so and whisper low

The Old Flag Never Touched the Ground

Words: James Weldon Johnson and Bob Cole
Music: Rosamond Johnson

When the cry came "off to war!"
To the front we proudly bore
Dear Old Glory and we followed it
Amidst the rattling of the rifles
And the cannon's roar
In the hail of shot and shell
Comrades all around us fell
But not once was lower'd in the dust, my boys
The der old flag we love so well

The old flag never touch'd the ground, boys
The old flag never touch'd the ground
Though shot and shell fell all around, boys
The dear old rag was never downed
The old flag never touch'd the ground, boys
Far to the front 'twas ever found
She's been in many a fix
Since seventeen seventy-six
But the old flag has never touched the ground

In the fiercest of the fight
Gleaming proudly in the light
At the front the Stars and Stripes
Were beck'ning us to strike
A manly blow for Freedom and for Right
Dear old flag! We bow to thee
Emblem of sweet Liberty
May you ever wave as you do now
A sign of peace and pow'r o'er land and sea

The Pussy and the Bow-Wow (1904)

Words: James Weldon Johnson
Music: Rosamond Johnson

SHE: I am a princess great and grand
And you are the son of a cook
HE: That's why I dare not take your hand
Nor even at you to look
SHE: But if I were a little pussy cat,
And you were a little bow-wow
HE: I'm sure we'd join in a social chat
In fact we'd have quite a little pow-wow

SHE: If I were a little pussy cat,
And you were a little bow-wow
HE: I know we wouldn't have to act
In the manner that we have to now
I'd bark my love
SHE: And Mine I'd mew
BOTH: As all good kitties and doggies do
SHE: If I were a little pussy cat
HE: And you were a little bow-wow.

HE: I wouldn't run you off the fence,
Nor chase you from out of the yard
SHE: To keep my claws from making dents in your face
I would try quite hard
HE: With my paw I would stroke your coat of silk
My collar, I'd let you wear it
SHE: I'd let you drink from my pan of milk,
And share my rug I declare it

Roll Them Cotton Bales (1914)

Words: James Weldon Johnson
Music by J. Rosamond Johnson

Down on the old Savannah river
All through the merry month of June
That's where the cotton am growing
Beneath the silvery southern moon
There's where the darkies am a sleeping
And all a-lying in a row
But every one is up and hustling
Soon as he hears the whistle blow
What's that noise so loud and clear?
Boo-woo! Boo-woo!
Seems to be a drawing near
Boo-woo! Boo-woo!
It sounds to me like the Robert E. Lee
Boo woo Boo woo
Chock full of cotton from Tennessee
Grab your truck and take your stand
For to roll them cotton bales

Roll them cotton bales
Roll 'em all the day
Roll them cotton bales
I'm goin' to roll them cotton bales
And roll 'em for my pay,
Yes, for my pay
Everybody better roll them cotton bales
Roll 'em down the line
Roll them cotton bales
I'm going to roll them cotton bales
For that gal of mine, that gal of mine
And just as soon as work is over

The money man will come around
I'll get my pay and then I'm ready
To see the sweetest gal in town
I'm working hard along the levee
So I can say to Lindy Lou
Do, honey tell me if you want me
Cause I'm just working gal for you
Boo woo! Boo woo!
It sounds to me like the Robert E. Lee
Boo woo Boo Woo
That means a dollar a day for me, Lindy Lou
It's all for you that I roll them cotton bales

NOTE: Handwritten on sheet music: "To Carl Van Vechten from
J. Rosamond Johnson: 'This was part of the original opening chorus
of our musical comedy 'The Red Moon.' I also introduced it in the
'Come Over Here Review' at the London Opera House, London,
England"

Run, Brudder Possum, Run (1900)

Words: James Weldon Johnson
Music: Rosamond Johnson

When de leaves begin to fall
You better run budder possum run
Mockin' bird commence to call
You better run brudder possum an' git out de way
You better run brudder possum an' git out de way
You better run somewhar an' hide
D'ole moon am sinkin' down behind de tree,
D'ole coon am thinkin' whar you gwinter to flee
D'ole dog am blinkin' and frisky az kin be
Yo chances I'm thinkin' look slim to me

You better run, run, run I tell you
Run brudder possum run
You better run, run, run I tell you
D'ole coon's got a gun
Young coons all gig-a-lin'
Cause dey knows dere's gwinter be some fun
You better run brudder possum an' git out de way
You better run brudder possum git out de way
You better run brudder possum an' git out de way
You better run brudder possum run

'Simmons ripenin' mighty fas'
You better run brudder possum run
Summer ain't gwine always las'
You better run brudder possum an' git out de way
You better run brudder possum an' git out de way
You better run somewhar an' hide
You sho' is cunnin' and you gittin' too fat
D'ole dog is runnin' right to whar yu'se at
D'ole coon is gunnin' jes lemme tell you dat
Tain't no time for funnin' so grab your hat

Mr. Possum take a tip
You better run brudder possum run,
Tain' no use in actin' flip
You better run brudder possum an' git out de way
You better run brudder possum an' git out de way
You better run somewhar an' hide
Dey gwine to houn' you all along de line,
When dey done foun' you, what de use in sigh'n
Wid tater roun' you sholy would tase fine,
Den fo' dey done groun' you jes git to fly'n

Sambo and Dinah (1904)

Words: Bob Cole and James Weldon Johnson
Music: Bob Cole

No doubt you've heard of Sambo,
The lad who plays the banjo,
And sings sweet songs to his dusky lady love
You've heard also of Dinah,
The gal from Carolina
With pearly teeth and eyes just like the stars above
Sup'pose you could be list'ning
While Dinah's eyes are glist'ning,
And Mister Sambo plunks his banjo, while he tries to woo;
Their love you'd hear them stammer,
Without respect to grammar,
For this is how those dusky lovers bill and coo
This is how these dusky lovers bill and coo

Sambo says to Dinah, "Does yo love me?"
Dinah says to Sambo, "Deed I do!"
Sambo says to Dinah, "Gal I wants you,"
Dinah says to Sambo, "I wants you too,"
Sambo says, "I'm feelin' kinder lonely,"
Dinah says, "I'm feelin' jes' de same,"
Sambo says, "Den tell me darlin' Dinah,
When you gwine to let me change yo' name."

Then Sambo with the banjo,
Says, "Does I understand yo',
To say you loves me as much as I love you?"
And she with heart a-pining,
Her teeth and eyes a-shining,
Says "Dats jes what I said and it am sho'ly true,"
Then Sambo says, "Oh! Dinah, no gal am mo' divinah,
You'se sweeter far to me dan honey in de honey comb"
"Don't talk so tantalizin'
Says Dinah "I'm surmisin'
You'se fixin' now to make me leave my happy home
Fixin' now to make me leave my happy home"

Save It For Me! (1903)

Words: James Weldon Johnson
Music: Bob Cole

Ephr'im Jones was bashful as he could be
When he'd go to court Miss Matilda Lee,
Ev'ry night to tell her his love he'd try
All he did was to stammer three words and sigh

If you've got a little empty corner in your heart,
Save it for me!
If you've got a little love and you can spare a part
Save it for me!
If you've got a little sympathy that you can share,
A little drop of pity, love, that you can spare,
Although it's but a "teeny" bit,
I don't care, won't you save it for me!

I don't dare to ask you for all your heart,
All I ask is just for a "teeny" part;
If with me, a little you will divide,
I will try my best to be satisfied

Sence You Went Away (1913)

Words: James Weldon Johnson
Music: J. Rosamond Johnson

Seems lak to me
De stars doan shine so bright
Seems lake to me
De sun done los' his light
Seems lak to me
De day's jes twice as long
Seems lak to me
De bird's forgot his song
Sence you went away

Seems lak to me
I jes can't help but sigh
Seems lak to me
A tear stays in my eye
Seems lak to me
I doan know what to do
Seems lak to me
Dat ev'ry thing wants you
Sence you went away

NOTE: Above the lyrics was written "Southern dialect Song"

James and Rosamond Johnson made their first trip to New York as songwriters during the summer of 1899. Although the comic opera they wrote and hoped to have produced was not presented on the stage, they met a number of key African-American individuals involved in show business, including the poet Paul Laurence Dunbar, who wrote in dialect. James Weldon Johnson had never written a dialect poem but, when he returned to Jacksonville, wrote "Sence You Went Away," which was published in the *Century* magazine. Later, Rosamond Johnson composed a melody for the poem and it was published as a song.

In his autobiography, James Weldon Johnson wrote "It was first sung by Amato, the Metropolitan Opera baritone; it was afterwards recorded for the phonography by John McCormack, with a violin obbligato played by Kreisler; and was again recorded by Louis Gravure and still again by Paul Robeson."

Since You Went Away

Words: James Weldon Johnson and Bob Cole
Music: J. Rosamond Johnson

Seems lak to me de stars don't shine so bright
Seems lak to me de sun done loss his light
Seems lak to me der's nothin' goin' right
Since you went away

Seems lake to me de sky ain't half so blue
Seems lak to me dat everything wants you
Seems lak to me I don't know what to do
Since you went away

Since you went a way, ma honey
Since you went a way, ma love
Worried night and day,ma honey
Since you went away ma dove!
Nothin' I can name, ma honey
Seems to me de same, somehow
Life ain't got no aim, ma honey,
Since you went away

Seems lak to me dat everything is wrong
Seems lak to me de day's jes' twice as long
Seems lak to me de bird's forgot his song
Since you went away
Seems lake to me I jes' can't help but sigh
Seems lak to me ma th'oat keeps gittin' dry
Seems lak to me a tear stays in my eye
Since you went away

NOTE: This is another version of "Sence You Went Away" with James Weldon Johnson and Bob Cole listed as the lyricists. The second version indicates the role that Bob Cole played in expanding the song.

The Soldier is the Idol of the Nation (1903)

Words: James Weldon Johnson
Music: Rosamond Johnson

When the band is playing its music so sweet
And the people cheering and crowding the street,
When the flags are flying gay
And the children stop their play,
While from ev'ry alley of the town they come;
When the girls are smiling and flashing their eyes
And the boys are filling the air with their cries
Then the gallant hero bold,
Clad in scarlet and in gold,
Marches to the tapping of the martial drum

The soldier is the idol of the nation,
When in his brilliant uniform arrayed,
He's an object fit for adoration
When he is out upon a dress parade;
Ev'ry heart with love for him is beating,
As he goes marching by the martial stride;
A hero peerless, a hero fearless,
He is the nation's pride

When the call to duty is heard on the air,
Summoning the soldier to do and to dare,
'Mid the cannon's thund'ring crush,
Where the swords like lightning flash,
To defend his country to the front he goes
When the fight is over and duty is done,
When the foe is vanquished, and vic't'ry is won
Back the gallant hero comes,
To the beating of the drums,
While the people greet him with a pride that glows

The soldier is the idol of the nation
When he returns from battle scarred and worn,
He's an object fit for adoration
Although his uniform is soiled and torn;
Ev'ry heart with love for him is beating,
As he goes marching by the martial stride;
A hero peerless, A hero fearless,
He is the nation's pride

Sounds of the Times: Lindy (1903)

Words: James Weldon Johnson
Music: Bob Cole and Rosamond Johnson

'Way down in sunny Louisiana
Down 'midst the fragrance of the banana
Down where the air with perfume is laden
There lives a charming dusky eyed Maiden
And when the little stars are a-peeling
'Round to her cabin door softly creeping
I go with my old banjo
And I sing to her this little song

Lindy! I am so lonely
And my poor heart seems for to want you only
I want you noontime, moontime, June-time
I want you all the time, my Lindy dear

Her manner keeps my mind in a-worry
Her coyness keeps my heart in a flurry
Sometimes she smiles upon me so sweetly
Sometimes she really cuts me completely
Maybe she does it only to tease me
Some day perhaps she will just to please me
Say that she'll name the day that
She will be my little honey wife

NOTE: Under the title on the sheet Music:

Farwell to the songs of by-gone days,
For now the air is laden
With syncopated notes in praise
Of some sweet dusky maiden
J. W. Johnson

The Spirit of the Banjo (1903)

Words: James Weldon Johnson and Bob Cole
Music: Rosamond Johnson

De silver moon am shinin'
De shadows round de cabin door am falling,
De katy did and a way up in the tree tops am a-calling
Across de fields of cotton, what is de sound we hear
A-tingling and a-jingling in tones so sweet and clear?
'Tis de music of de banjo dat's a-floatin' on de air
De music of de banjo dat's a-floatin' on de air
De music of de banjo dat's a-floatin' on de air
De music of de banjo dat's a-floatin' on de air

All thoo' the evenin'
De music of de banjo is a-floatin' on de breeze
Tinglin' and a-jinglin'
It comes across the fields and thoo the trees
Banjo a-ringin'
De darkies cuttin' capers up and down de cabin flo'
Wingin' and singin' to the music of de old banjo

Oh! Everything is beatin' to de music dat de banjo is a-makin'
From de cotton blossoms wavin'
To de feet dat keep de cabin flo' a-shakin'
It ain't de strings and fingers dat makes yo' heart to beat
Dat keep yo' hands a-clappin' and makes you move ya feet
It's de spirit of de banjo dat's what makes de music sweet
De spirit of de banjo, dat's what makes de music sweet
De spirit of de banjo, dat's what makes de music sweet
De spirit of de banjo, dat's what makes de music sweet

Sweet Saloma (Serenade)

Words: Bob Cole and James Weldon Johnson
Music: Rosamond Johnson

Slumber on, but dream of me
White I sing, my love, to thee
A sweet romanza:

Sweet Saloma art thou dreaming,
While I lift my soul in song to thee
Sweet Saloma while the stars are gleaming
Dost thou ever dream of me!
Sleep on my sweet Saloma
Where e'er your fancies lead you
Through dreamland where they speed you
There would I also be
Sleep on my sweet Saloma
And even in thy sleeping
My heart is in thy keeping
Slumber on but dream of me

Golden moonbeams gently falling,
And the silv'ry stars shine but for thee
All the voices of the night are calling
Telling you to dream of me
Sleep on my sweet Saloma
Where e'er your fancies lead you
Through dreamland where they speed you
There would I also be
Sleep on my sweet Saloma
And even in thy sleeping
My heart is in thy keeping
Slumber on but dream of me

Tell Me, Dusky Maiden

Words: James Weldon Johnson and Bob Cole
Music: Rosamond Johnson

BOYS: Howdy do, I have for you
A special invitation to a swell affair
And I've been thinking my dusky maiden
That I might escort you there
GIRLS: You're a stranger to me and I really can't see
Why you should show such impropriety
This my mama must know
BOYS: Then to mama we'll go
GIRLS: But suppose that mama dear says no
BOYS: Then tell me, tell me dusky maiden
GIRLS: "All coons look alike to me"
BOYS: If I plight to you my love
GIRLS: Just because I made dem goo goo eyes
BOYS: Will you be my little turtle dove?
GIRLS: Well, I don't know
BOYS: Maiden believe me
I really mean what I say
Won't you name the day?
GIRLS: Excuse me
BOYS: When shall I call for my answer?
GIRLS Ah! When you ain't got no money
Well, you need'nt come around
BOYS: I understand you
GIRLS: I think I'll give you a trial
Since you will take no denial
If you deceive me
I don't know what on earth I'll do
BOYS: I'll not deceive you
I'll be true my love
GIRLS: Come then and take a little walk

And then we'll have a little talk
And maybe you and I will see
Just what our future life will be
BOYS: You will see how happy we will be
GIRLS: I'll peruse, sir, if you choose,
This special invitation to a swell affair
And if I find that it will be proper
Then you may escort me
BOYS: You can readily see
'Tis a pleasure to me
To satisfy your curiosity
GIRLS: But if mama says no?
BOYS: I don't care, we will go
GIRLS: Oh, I tho't you'd like to have her know
BOYS: Then tell me tell me dusky stranger
GIRLS: "All girls look alike to me"
BOYS: If I give you all my love
GIRLS: Just because I made dem goo goo eyes
BOYS: Shall I be your only turtle dove
GIRLS: Well I don't know
BOYS: Stranger, believe me
I really mean
Now just as soon as you bring a nice diamond ring
GIRLS: Excuse me
BOYS: Then you may call for your answer
GIRLS: Ah! 'Spose I ain't got no diamond,
Then I need'nt come around
BOYS: Oh, I was teasing
GIRLS: I think I'll give you a trial
Since you will take no denial
If you deceive me
I don't know what on earth I'll do
BOYS: I'll not deceive you

GIRLS: Come then and take a little walk
And then we'll have a little talk
BOYS: I'll be true, my love, to you
GIRLS: And maybe you and I will see,
Just what our future life will be
BOYS: You will see how happy we can be

There's a Very Pretty Moon To-night (1903)

Words: James Weldon Johnson
Music: Rosamond Johnson

There is a time for love and wooing
When nature lends her aid
There is a time for heart's undoing,
When Cupid's plots are laid;
'Tis when the moon with gentle magic
Puts ev'ry heart in tune
Tonight she shines in all her splendor
Come out beneath the moon

The moon is out in all her glory
She sheds her tender ray;
Come, let me tell you love's old story,
Beneath her mystic sway,
The night bird's voice is softly calling
The lazy breezes croon
It is a night for love and lovers
Come out beneath the moon

There's a very pretty moon tonight, love,
There's an invitation on the breeze
There's a welcome in the winking of the stars, love,
There seems to come a beck'ning from the trees
There's a very pretty moon tonight, love,
Come and stroll beneath her silv'ry light
'Tis the time for lovers vows and lovers pleadings,
For there's a very pretty moon tonight

NOTE: In early 1903 the producers Klaw and Erlanger brought *Mother Goose* to the United States from London, where it had been a success on Drury Lane. Cole and the Johnson brothers wrote six songs for the musical, which was presented as an extended production number called "The Evolution of Ragtime." The Johnson's best song in that production was the beautiful ballad, "There's a Very Pretty Moon To-Night."

There's Something About You, That I Love, Love Love (1904)

Words: James Weldon Johnson
Music: Bob Cole

Some girls may be just as pretty,
Some may be as neat;
Others may be far more witty,
But there's none so sweet,
Yet why I call you the sweetest,
I can't tell though I often try
You make my joy the completest
But I can't tell why

There is something about you,
That I love, love, love
And I can't do without you
You're my turtle dove;
'Round my heart you're fitted
As closely as a glove,
There is something about you
That I love, love, love

Is it the color or glances
Of your tender eyes?
Is it your smile that entrances
Or your gentle sighs?
Is it the shade of your tresses
Or the size of your little feet,
Or just the style of your dresses
Makes you seem so sweet?

Treat Me Like a Baby Doll (1914)

Word: James Weldon Johnson
Music: J. Rosamond Johnson

You want to know—you tell me so
My precious angel boy
How you can thrill my soul and fill
My heart with perfect joy
You say you yearn sweetheart to learn
Just what you ought to do
My heart to take and how to make me
Love you fond and true

Treat me like a baby doll
Hold me tight, don't let me fall
Just take and place me on your knee
And make a fuss love over me
Squeeze me till I say "pa-pa"
Press me and caress me
Ah, just treat me sweetly, do it neatly
And kiss me into bliss completely
Treat me, treat me like a baby doll

When we're alone, my dearest own,
Pick out a comfy chair,
Lower the light, cuddle me tight
But handle me with care
Draw me up near, call me your dear
And ride me on your knee
If I should sigh, or I should cry
Use baby talk to me

Treat me like a baby doll
Hold me tight, don't let me fall
Just take and place me on your knee
And make a fuss love over me
Squeeze me till I say "pa-pa"
Press me and caress me
Ah, just treat me sweetly, do it neatly
And kiss me into bliss completely
Treat me, treat me like a baby doll

Two Eyes (1903)

Words: James Weldon Johnson
Music: Rosamond Johnson

There are two eyes
To which the sun
Cannot new luster lend,
Two eyes in which the midnight
And the starlight softly blend,
Two eyes in which the depths of love
Are deeper than the sea
Ah! If the love that in them lies
Were only there for me;
Ah! If the love that in them lies
Were only there for me

Under the Bamboo Tree (1902)

Words and Music: Bob Cole

Down in the jungles lived a maid
Of royal blood though dusky shade
A marked impression once she made
Upon a Zulu from Ma-ta-boo-loo
And ev'ry morning he would be
Down underneath a bamboo tree
Awaiting there, his love to see
And then to her he'd sing

If you lak-a me, lak I lak-a-you
And we lak-a-both the same
I lak-a say, this very day
I lak-a-change your name
Cause I love a-you and love a-you true
And if you-a love me too
One live as two, two live as one
Under the bamboo tree

And in this simple jungle way
He wooed the maiden ev'ry day
By singing what he had to say
One day he seized her and gently squeezed her
And then beneath the bamboo green
He begged her to become his queen
The dusky maiden blushed unseen
And joined him in his song
This little story strange but true

Is often told in Ma-ta-boo,
Of how this Zulu tried to woo
His jungle lady in topics shady
Although the scene was miles away
Right here at home I dare to say
You'll hear some Zulu ev'ry day,
Gush out this soft refrain

NOTE: Bob Cole is the only writer listed, although James Weldon Johnson stated that the song was a group effort. The song, sung by Marie Cahill in *Sally In Our Alley* in 1902, was Cole and the Johnson brothers biggest hit. The song originated with Rosamond Johnson using the chorus of the old spiritual, "Nobody Knows The Trouble I've Seen" to begin the song. It was sung by Marie Cahill for years, first recorded by Arthur Collins and Byron Harlan. This was the first of a long line of "jungle songs" from Tin Pan Alley. Later, it was featured in the 1944 film *Meet Me in St. Louis* starring Judy Garland.

What It Takes To Make Me Love You, You've Got It (1904)

Words: James Weldon Johnson
Music: James Reese Europe

What makes me love you the way I do,
What makes me linger and long for you?
What can it be dearie, what can it be?
Really, I want to see through this great mystery dearie.
I find in you what I miss elsewhere,
Something that draws me and holds me there,
The lure, the call, that makes me fall,
Sweet Baby Doll, you've got it all

You've got the kind of kiss that always makes me sigh
Got the sort of something 'bout you makes me want to die
Got the loving look that makes me oh so glad,
Fills me, thrills me, drives me mad
You've got the naughty way of saying Sweetie dear
Always seem to want me when I cuddle near
What it takes to make me love you
You've got it!
Sweetheart, you've got it.

Sometimes I hardly know what to do,
With all the sweetness I find in you,
That is no "con" dearie, to you I'm drawn, really,
You've got me gone when you turn it all on, dearie.
You've got my heart and my soul aflame,
Nobody else, makes me feel the same,
For you inspire, love's sweet desire,
You touch the wire that starts the fire.

You've got the kind of kiss that always makes me sigh
Got the sort of something 'bout you makes me want to die
Got the loving look that makes me oh so glad,
Fills me, thrills me drives me mad
You've got the naughty way of saying Sweetie dear
Always seem to want me when I cuddle near
What it takes to make me love you
You've got it!
Sweetheart, you've got it.

When De Jack O'Lantern Starts to Walk About (1901)

Words: Bob Cole and James Weldon Johnson
Music: Rosamond Johnson

When de ole moon is a-wastin' an' a gittin' out de way
Den de Jack O'lantern starts to walk about;
'Twixt de settin' ob de sun an' de breakin' ob de day
Den de Jack o'lantern starts to walk about
When de wind it is a moanin' an' a sighin' thro' de pines,
An' de owl he is a-hootin' an' de dogs begin to whine
An' de tree frog is a singin' it's a pretty sure sign
Dat de Jack o'lantern gwine-ter walk about

Ev'ry pickaninny must be tucked in bed;
Not a pickaninny should be out
Ev'ry one must cover up his little wooley head,
When de Jack o'lantern starts to walk about!
Ev'ry pickaninny must be fast asleep
In his trundle bed without a doubt
And from under neath the cover he should never peep
When de Jack o'lantern starts to walk about!

Lemme tell you pickaninnies you had better all be good
When de Jack o'lantern starts to walk about
Better stop dat stealin' melons an' act jes' like you should,
When de Jack o'lantern stars to walk about
Now de Jack o'lantern chillum, is a sorter curious light,
Fust it springs upon yo' lef' den it springs upon yo right
But if you try to catch it, you will follow it all night,
When de Jack o'lantern starts to walk about

When It's All Goin' Out, And Nothin' Comin' In (1902)

Words and Music: Bert Williams and George Walker
Words revised by James Weldon Johnson

Money is de root of evil
No matter where you happen to go
But nobody has any objections
To de root, now ain't dat so?
You know how it is wid money
How it makes you feel at ease
De world puts on a big broad smile
An' yo' friends am as thick as bees
But, Oh! When yo' money is runnin' low
An' you'se clinging to a solitary dime
Yo' creditors are num'rous an' yo friends are few
Oh, dat am de awful time

Dat am de time, Oh dat am de time
When it's all goin' out, and nothin' comin' in
Dat am de time when de troubles begin
Money's gittin' low, people say "I told you so"
And you can't borrow a penny from any of yo' kin
An' it's all goin' out, an' nothin' comin' in

Dat am de time when de troubles begin
Money's gittin' low, people say "I told you so"
And you can't borrow a penny from any of yo' kin
An' it's all goin' out an' nothin' comin' in

Had my share of dis world's trials
Nobody knows how hard I have tried
To keep my little boat from sinkin'
An' to battle wid de tide
You know when you've got yo' money
You kin easy keep afloat
De stream is smooth an' all yo' friends
Tries to help you to row yo' boat
But, Oh! When yo' money is runnin' low
An' de stream gits rough,
An' things look mighty blue
Yo' look around for help an' find
Each of yo' friends is paddlin' his own canoe

Dat am de time, Oh, dat am de time
When it's all goin' out an' nothin' comin' in

Dat am de time when de troubles begin
Money's gittin' low, people say "I told you so"
And you can't borrow a penny from any of yo' kin
An' it's all goin' out an' nothin' comin' in

NOTE: This song was in the Williams and Walker musicals *Sons of Ham* and *In Dahomey*, then interpolated in *Sally in Our Alley*, starring Marie Cahill. It was recorded by Bert Williams for Victor Records in 1901.

When the Band Plays Ragtime (1904)

Words: James Weldon Johnson
Music: Bob Cole

Talk about the music of your Sousa
And of all the other famous bands
If they're playing music that is classic
People sit and simply clap their hands
But you see the folks commence a-smiling
When the band hits up a ragtime tune
By the tapping of the drum,
You can tell it's going to come
And your feet will be a-moving pretty soon

When the band plays ragtime
Every body sings
When the band plays ragtime
It sets your feet on springs
When the band plays ragtime
You feel like you've got wings
I declare you jes can't he'p it,
You've jes got to kinder step it,
When the band plays ragtime

There's no earthly use in talking 'bout it
Though some high-toned people call it rot
They all have to own up when they hear it
That it hits a mighty ticklish spot
It may not be very good for brain food
But the heart is where it touches you
And it makes you want to dance
And you feel like you could prance
Oh, it seems to do you good all through and through

Why Don't the Band Play? (1900)

Words: Bob Cole and James Weldon Johnson
Music: Rosamond Johnson

Strolling through the park, out upon a lark
With your sweet Verbena by your side;
Plighting vows of love, by the stars above,
Swearing you'll be true what-e'er betide
If the maid demure, feeling rather sure
That your love would not forever flame,
Suddenly should say, "Let us name the day!"
You'd feel an inclination to exclaim,

Why don't the band play a lively tune?
Make it a loud one, and play it soon;
Why don't they beat the big bass drum,
With a loud ta-rum ta-rum?
Oh, why don't the band play a lively tune?

On some other night, when the moon is bright
And the stars are twinkling in the skies
In the same old way, same old things you say,
Gazing in each other's same old eyes
Flirting days have fled, time has come to wed,
And the gentle maiden you implore,
"Won't you be my wife?" "Not upon your life!"
Why use that same expression as before?

Many years have passed, married life at last,
Seems to rob you of those single joys;
And the same old dodge, going to the lodge,
Gives you chance to get out with the boys
Coming home quite late, on that same old skate,
Latch-key will not find its proper place
Wifey says, "ta, ta! Going back to Ma."
Well, how would this expression suit the case?

Why don't the band play a lively tune?
Make it a loud one, and play it soon;
Why don't they beat the big bass drum,
With a loud ta-rum ta-rum?
Oh, why don't the band play a lively tune?

Won't Your Mama Let You Come Out and Play? (1906)

Words: James Weldon Johnson
Music: Bob Cole

Won't your Mama let you come out
And play a little while
Little girl, with a nice little boy?

How am I to know you are a nice little boy?
How am I to know you'll not be naughty?
How am I to know, Sir, that you will behave yourself?
Said the little maiden haughty

Most every little girl who's been to play with me
Said I was as nice as any little boy could be
Won't you come out to play, and may be you'll agree
That the other boys are not like me

Little girl, little girl,
Won't your Mama let you come out and play?
Little girl, little girl
I've a lot of things to you I want to say
What would you like to have me do?
I'll do most anything for you
'Cause I like you thro' and thro' little girl,
Won't your Mama let you come out and play?
Little girl, won't your Mama let you come out and play?

If you've never been out playing
Sometimes with little boys
Don't you know that you've missed lots of fun?

Mama always told me little boys were so rude
That their names weren't the best precisely
So suppose I should come out and play awhile with you
Are you sure you'd act quite nicely?

I'd show you just how nice it is to play with boys
I would share my candy, and I'd share my newest toys
I'd show you all the fun a little boy enjoys
Won't you come along and play with me?

You Go Your Way And I'll Go Mine (1915)

Words: James Weldon Johnson
Music: J. Rosamond Johnson

I gave you all the love I had
In turn you gave me none
You stole your way into my soul
And when my love was won
Just as soon as that was done
You wrung my heart
You made it bleed and now we part
You go your way and I'll go mine
And please don't think that
I'm a-going to waste away and pine
I'm going to want you, I know that's true
Believe me, Honey, you're going to want me too
That soothing love you've got is just the kind
That satisfied the longing of this heart of mine
I know I'll miss that burning kiss
For it traveled to my head like wine
My heart will ache, my heart might break
Yet still I say, you go your way and I'll go mine

Our skies of love, I thought they'd be
Forever bright and clear
But ev'ry smile has cost a sigh
And ev'ry kiss a tear,
Yet I can't forget you dear, you've made me cry
But still I had to say good-bye

James Weldon Johnson

NOTE: James Weldon Johnson joined the diplomatic service and became Consul in Venezuela in 1906; he was later transferred to Nicaragua but in 1913 returned to the United States because the Democratic administration of Woodrow Wilson wanted to reward Democrats with patronage and Johnson, a Republican, knew that his future in the diplomatic corps was bleak. On the sheet music to this song, Rosamond Johnson noted the song was "written after Jim came back from South America—the last popular song we wrote together."

– 186 –

You're All Right, Teddy (1904)

Words and Music: Cole and Johnson

The country calls again
For true and honest men
To vote to save its honor and its fame
So let us all unite
And cast our ballots right
For Teddy Roosevelt
The man we name

Oh! You are all right, Teddy!
You're the kind that we remember;
Don't you worry!
We are with you!
You're all right, Teddy!
And we'll prove it in November, Teddy!
We're going to keep you in the White House

Oh, Teddy is a man,
That's built upon a plan
To make the hearts of plucky men rejoice;
For when the game begins,
He goes right in and wins,
And that is why he is the people's choice.

Oh! You're a man indeed,
The kind of man we need,
The kind of man we need to hold the gap;
You've steered the country straight,
You've made the country great,
 In fact, you've put the country on the map.

And when the country's cry
For men to fight and die
Resounded through the land from Washington,
Then Teddy didn't stop to talk
But went and did his work at San Juan.

When Europe raised a fuss,
And tried to say to us:
"What? Dig through Panama, you never shall!"
Our Teddy said: "All right!
I'll think it over for a night."
Next day we got the Panama Canal.

NOTE: This was a campaign song written for Teddy Roosevelt for the 1904 election. The most popular tune during the Roosevelt campaign was "A Hot Time in the Old Town Tonight."

You's Sweet To Yo' Mammy Jes' The Same (1911)

Words: James Weldon Johnson
Music: J. Rosamond Johnson

Shet yo' eyes, ma little pickaninny, go to sleep
Mammy's watchin' by you all the w'ile
Daddy is a woik-in' way down in the cott'n fiel'
He's woik-in' fo' his little honey chile
An' yo' Mammy's heart is jes a brimmin' full o' lov'
Fo' you f'om yo' haid down to yo' tiny feet
Oh! No mattah wat some othah folks may say an' think o' you,
To yo' Mammy's heart you sho' am mighty sweet

You's sweet to yo' Mammy jes the same
Da's why I calls you honey fo' yo' name
Yo' face is black da's true
An' yo' hair is wooley too,
But you's sweet to yo' Mammy jes the same

Up dere in the big house,
W'ere dey live so rich an' gran'
Dey's got chillum dat dey luv's I s'pose
Chillun dat am purty
Oh! But dey can't love 'em mo'
Dan yo' ole Mammy lov's you, heav'n knows!
Dey may think you's homely
An' yo' clo'es dey may be po'
But yo' shinin' eyes, dey hol's fo' me a light
Dat ma little honey w'en you opens dem so big an' roun'
Makes you lov'ly in yo' dear ole Mammy's sight

The Young Warrior (1915)

Words: James Weldon Johnson (Italian text by Edoardo Petri)
Music: H. T. Burleigh

Mother, shed no mournful tears,
But gird me on my sword;
And give no utterance to thy fears
But bless me with thy word
Now, let thine eyes my way pursue
Where'er my footsteps fare;
And when they lead beyond thy view,
Send them after me a prayer

Still, pray not to defend from harm,
Nor danger to dispel,
But rather that with steadfast arm
I fight the battle well

Pray that I keep, through all the days,
My heart and purpose strong
My sword unsullied, and always
Unsheathed against the wrong

The lines are drawn, the fight is on,
A cause is to be won;
Mother, look not so white and wan,
Give Godspeed to thy son

NOTE: From: The musical Critic of the New York Tribune, February 28, 1916:

"An interesting feature was the singing of Mr. Amato of an Italian patriotic song written by an American Negro. This was Harry T. Burleigh's "Il Giovane Guerriero" and it proved to be the sensation of the evening. It was a splendidly spirited martial song, and ought to thrill many an Italian crowd in after years. That an American Negro could write such a song seems strange indeed. It is one of the few really admirable songs America has produced in recent years. All honor to Harry T. Burleigh!"

In Italy the song has produced such an effect that Maestro R. Zandonai, one of Italy's greatest operatic composers of the present day has consented to furnish the orchestration for the song to be performed all over Italy—truly a great honor for this American Composer.

Your Eyes So Deep (1915)

Words: James Weldon Johnson
Music: Harry T. Burleigh

Your eyes so deep and tender are
Soft with the glamour of a star,
Bright with the gentle light that lies
In placid streams and sunny skies;
Your eyes so tender are
And yet, those melting smiling eyes,
From out their depths so sweet,
Have lanced a cruel, piercing dart;
And now my wounded, bleeding heart
Lies captive at your feet
Your lips are like a sweet red rose
That in some scented garden grows,
A dewy rose, so sweet and red,
That blooms amidst a lily bed
Your lips are like a rose:
And yet those velvet petal'd lips
A honey'd poison brew
That thro' my veins has run like fire
And fill'd my soul with love's desire
And left me mad for you
For you

Your Lips Are Wine (1915)

Words: James Weldon Johnson
Music: H.T. Burleigh

Your lips are wine,
O Heart's Desire
Give me the flame
Of their passion kindling fire
The world melts away
In the glow of your kiss
And leaves just you and me
Alone in silent bliss
Your lips again
Give them to mine
One more full draught
Of their nectar'd anodyne
In the fold of your arms
Lull me softly, softly
Until there comes
The wondrous calm
The calm of love so deep and still

Zels Zels (Arabian Love Song) (1905)

Words: James Weldon Johnson
Music: Bob Cole

Way off in Bizerta Land
Near the burning desert sand
Hid behind her lattice shade,
Lived a lovely Moorish maid
Selah! Selah!

So fair, so fair was she
But an Arab chieftain bold
Chanced her beauty to behold
One spark from her fleeting gaze
Set his Arab heart ablaze
Selah! Selah!

In love, in love was he
One night his steed bestriding
Across the desert riding
Love's star his courser guiding
This chieftain rode to woo
He rode, he rode,
And sang while on he rode

Zel-Zel! My oriental belle!
How love you no one can tell,
My belle of the Orient!
Come to my bungalow and dwell
Zel-Zel! My oriental belle!

On his steed so fleet and strong,
Fast this chieftain sped along
Till at last his course he stayed
Neath the window of the maid
Selah! Selah!

In haste to woo was he
There he told her of his love
Swore by all the stars above
But although his love he proved
She appeared to be unmoved
Selah! Selah!

So coy, so coy was she
It seemed that she grew colder
The more of love he told her
But he at last grew bolder
And seized her in his arms
Then back he rode
And sang while on he rode

Works Cited

1. Johnson, James Weldon. *Black Manhattan.* New York: Atheneum, 1968. (From Studies in American Negro Life, August Meier, General Editor), p. 114
2. Jasen, David A. and Gene Jones. *Spreadin' Rhythm Around: Black Popular Songwriters, 1880-1930.* New York: Schirmer, 1998, p. 32
3. Johnson, James Weldon. *Along This Way: The Autobiography of James Weldon Johnson.* New York, Penguin, 1933; copyright renewed, 1961, p. 177
4. Abbott, Lynn and Doug Seroff. *Ragged But Right: Black Traveling Shows, "Coon Songs," and the Dark Pathway to Blues and Jazz.* Jackson: University Press of Mississippi, 2007, quoted , p. 37.
5. Jasen & Jones, p 41
6. Ibid, p.
7. Forbes, Camille F. *Introducing Bert Williams: Burnt Cork, Broadway, and the Story of America's First Black Star.* New York: Basic Books, 2008, p. 30
8. Ibid, p. 34
9. Johnson, *Along This Way*, p. 176
10. Ibid, p. 176
11. Ibid, p. 177
12. Ibid, p. 177
13. Ibid, p. 177
14. Jasen and Jones, p. 98
15. Ibid, p. 98
16. Ibid p. 98-99
17. Johnson, *Along This Way*, p. 152
18. Ibid, p. 155
19. Ibid, p. 156-157
20. Ibid, p. 161

21. Ibid p. 159
22. Johnson, James Weldon and J. Rosamond Johnson. *The Books of American Negro Spirituals* (Two Volumes in One) New York: Da Capo Press, 1925, 1926 by Viking Press. P. 42
23. Ibid, p. 44
24. Johnson, *Along This Way*, pp 172-173
25. Ibid 173-174
26. Jasen and Jones, pp 108-109
27. Johnson, *Along This Way*, p. 178
28. Ibid, p. 186
29. Ibid, p. 189
30. Norrell, Robert J. *Up From History: The Life of Booker T. Washington*. Cambridge, MA: The Belknap Press of Harvard University Press, 2009, p. 6
31. Johnson, *Along This Way* p. 221
32. Ibid, p. 222
33. Ibid, p. 223
34. Ibid, p. 222
35. Badger, Reid. *A Life in Ragtime: A Biography of James Reese Europe*. New York: Oxford University Press, 1995, p. 20
36. Ibid, p. 26
37. Ibid, p. 31
38. Ibid, p. 34
39. Badger, p. 39
40. Jasen and Jones, p. 112-113
41. Ibid, p. 114
42. Ibid, p. 114
43. Ibid, p. 95
44. Ibid, p. 95
45. James Weldon Johnson files at the Bienecke Library

Bibliography

Abbott, Lynn and Doug Seroff. *Out of Sight: The Rise of African American Popular Music 1889-1895*. Jackson: University Press of Mississippi, 2002.

Abbott, Lynn and Doug Seroff. *Ragged But Right: Black Traveling Shows, "Coon Songs," and the Dark Pathway to Blues and Jazz*. Jackson: University Press of Mississippi, 2007.

Badger, Reid. *A Life in Ragtime: A Biography of James Reese Europe*. New York: Oxford University Press, 1995.)

Brooks, Tim. *Lost Sounds: Blacks and the Birth of the Recording Industry, 1890-1919*. Urbana and Chicago: University of Illinois Press, 2004

Dennison, Sam. *Scandalize My Name: Black Imagery in American Popular Music*. New York: Garland, 1982.

Floyd, Samuel A. Jr. *The Power of Black Music: Interpreting Its History From Africa to the United States*. New York: Oxford University Press, 1995.

Forbes, Camille F. *Introducing Bert Williams: Burnt Cork, Broadway, and the Story of America's First Black Star*. New York: Basic Books, 2008.)

Goldman, Herbert G. *Jolson: The Legend Comes To Life*. New York: Oxford University Press, 1988.

Gullickson, Luke. "Presidential Campaign Songs of the Progressive Era: The Political Language of Personality," *Constructing the Past*: Vol. 8; Issue 1, Article 4.

Huggins, Nathan Irvin. *Harlem Renaissance*. New York: Oxford University Press, 1971.

Jasen, David A. and Gene Jones. *Spreadin' Rhythm Around: Black Popular Songwriters, 1880-1930*. New York: Schirmer Books, 1998.

Johnson, James Weldon and J. Rosamond Johnson. *The Books of American Negro Spirituals* (Two Volumes in One) New York:

Da Capo Press, 1925, 1926 by Viking Press.

Johnson, James Weldon. *Along This Way: The Autobiography of James Weldon Johnson*. New York, Penguin, 1933; copyright renewed, 1961.

Johnson, James Weldon. *Black Manhattan*. New York: Atheneum, 1968. (From Studies in American Negro Life, August Meier, General Editor)

Levy, Eugene. *James Weldon Johnson: Black Leader, Black Voice*. Chicago: The University of Chicago Press, 1973.

Lewis, David Levering. *W.E.B. DuBois: Biography of a Race: 1868-1919*. New York: Henry Holt and Company, 1993.

Lewis, David Levering. *When Harlem Was in Vogue*. New York: Penguin Books, 1979, 1981, 1997.

Locke, Alain, editor. *The New Negro: Voices of the Harlem Renaissance*. New York: Atheneum, 1992.

Mahar, William J. *Behind the Burnt Cork Mask: Early Blackface Minstrelsy and Antebellum American Popular Culture*. Urbana and Chicago: University of Illinois Press, 1999.

Norrell, Robert J. *Up From History: The Life of Booker T. Washington*. Cambridge, MA: The Belknap Press of Harvard University Press, 2009.)

Quarles, Benjamin. *The Negro in the Making of America*, Third Edition. New York: Touchstone, 1964, 1969, 1987.

Silber, Irwin. *Songs America Voted By*. Harrisburg, PA: Stackpole Books, 1971.

Work, John W., Lewis Wade Jones, and Samuel C. Adams, Jr. *Lost Delta Found: Rediscovering the Fisk University-Library of Congress Coahoma County Study, 1941-1942*. Robert Gordon and Bruce Nemerov, Editors. Nashville: Vanderbilt University Press, 2005.

Wynn, Neil A. Editor. *Cross the Water Blues: African American Music in Europe*. Jackson: University Press of Mississippi, 2007.

Index